BIG BURN
The Northwest's Great Forest Fires of 1910

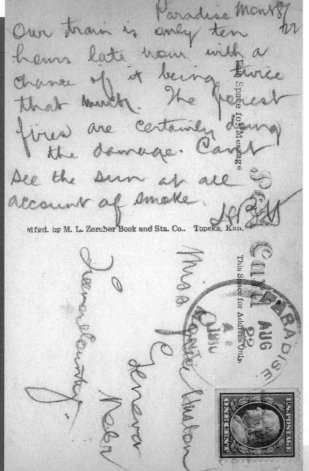

Paradise Mont

Our train is only ten hours late now with a chance of it being twice that much. The forest fires are certainly doing the damage. Can't see the sun at all account of smoke.

Mfgd. by M. L. Zercher Book and Sta. Co., Topeka, Kan.

This Space for Message

This Space for Address Only.

On this card, post-marked "Paradise, Mont., Aug. 22, 1910" a traveler tells of delays encountered because of the forest fire season of 1910.

222. N. P. Tunnel Cut-off, Paradise, Montana
Published by Paradise Drug Store

Fire Fiercest in 1910 Death Trap

The fiercest fury of the fire near Avery, Idaho, is in the spot where 28 fire-fighters were burned to death in 1910, it is said by the Forest Service. These men were part of a crew of 70 which stopped on Setzer creek to have supper. The ranger in charge of the fire crews sent a man named Charles Sullivan, deputy sheriff at Avery, to warn them away from the encroaching flames.

Most of the men left hurriedly, but 28 asserted that they would wait for supper, fire or no fire. They sat down to their meal as the holocaust struck them. Not one was left alive, all being burned and charred so badly as to be unrecognizable. The bodies were wrapped in blankets and heavy burlap and buried there. Later they were disinterred and removed to the St. Maries, Idaho, cemetery for fire-fighters.

The young U.S. Forest Service was baptized with fire in 1910. The "Big Burn of 1910" was the most disastrous fire ever recorded in the Northern Region.

The
BIG BURN
The Northwest's Great
Forest Fires
of 1910

by Don Miller
and
Stan Cohen

To Jack
Best Wishes
in Wallace
Stan Cohen
8-21-10

LIBRARY OF CONGRESS CATALOG
CARD NUMBER 78-51507

ISBN 978-0-933126-04-6

First Printing 1978
Second Printing 1980
Third Printing, Revised 1993
Fourth Printing, Revised 2001
Fifth Printing, Revised 2010

Typography and layout by Jan Taylor
on Macintosh utilizing:
Aldus Pagemaker 6.5
Adobe Photoshop 5.0

Cover Graphics by Mike Egler, Egler Designs

Printed in Canada

PICTORIAL HISTORIES PUBLISHING COMPAMY, INC.
713 South Third West, Missoula, Montana 59801
(406) 549-8488   phpc@montana.com
www.pictorialhistoriespublishing.com

Introduction

The year 1910 was a strange one for many people in northern Idaho and western Montana. The superstitious and some of the religious saw portents of weird, calamitous events to come as fiery Haley's Comet zoomed on spectacular paths across the heavens.

Those who believed that disasters came with some regularity searched for a pattern. Their thoughts went west, pondering the 1846 Yaquina fire in Oregon which burned 450,000 acres of prime timber. Three other fires in Oregon haunted them: the Nestucca in which 320,000 acres were burned on the Oregon coast in 1853, the Silverton fire of 1865 which claimed one million acres, and the Coos fire, which consumed over 300,000 acres in September and October 1868.

To the south in Wyoming, one–half million acres had been ravished in the Bighorn fire of 1876, and to the east had been the debilitating Peshtigo, Wisconsin, conflagration of October 9, 1871. About 1,280,000 acres were destroyed, and 1,182 people perished. While the Peshtigo fire roared, so, too, did the great Chicago fire of October 8-11, caused by a burning lantern knocked over by Mrs. O'Leary's cow. In 1881, voracious forest fires in Michigan destroyed one million acres of timber and snuffed out 138 lives.

Freshest in people's minds was the September 1, 1894, fire which burned in and around Hinckley, Minnesota, obliterating 160,000 acres, and killing 413 people.

A good case could be made for predicting a calamitous forest fire that would ravage the heretofore relatively unscathed, lush timber stands of the Northwest. Other people shrugged and lamented that one could never predict much of the future because Lady Luck was so damnably fickle.

Regardless of what people thought, or feared, or guessed—or didn't bother to think or fear or guess—1910 was to be the year of what some termed the "big blowup" or the "big burn" or the "time when the mountains roared."

It was a series of 1,736 fires that ravaged three million acres and killed 85 (possibly 87) people, particularly during August 20 and 21—the two most grueling days of searing hell. The undermanned, underequipped national forests did not help the situation. With abnormally low amounts of precipitation and soaring, high temperatures, disaster threatened imminently.

The authors

Acknowledgments

Many people contributed to the completion of the first printing of this book in 1978. Beverly Ayers, former photo librarian, Administrative Services of the Northern Region, provided most of the photos from the Forest Service archives. Jack Byrne of Missoula provided pictures of DeBorgia from his grandfather's collection. Hank Kottkey of Wallace, who was born in Wallace August 9, 1910, and whose father was the ranger at Avery in 1910, provided pictures given to his father by Ranger Joe Halm. Hank was evacuated to Missoula August 20. He spent 40 years with the Forest Service before retiring in 1967. Bob Mutch, a long-time Forest Service employee in fire control and research reviewed the text for technical accuracy. Dianne Kedro of Boulder, Colorado, edited the manuscript. A special thanks to Jud Moore and Gail Uber of Region One's Public Affairs office.

For the present 2001 printing, thanks again to the staff of the Public Affairs& Government Relations Office for the loan of photos and especially to Rob Stanton. The Harry English photos are courtesy of the Historic Wallace Preservation Society, Inc., with additional photos from the Special Collections, University of Idaho library, Barnard Stockbridge Collection. Dave Strohmaier provided photos of some of the existing grave site monuments, and a special thanks to John Amonson of the Wallace District Mining Museum for his help and encouragement with this new edition. James Buckham kindly gave permission to use his mural on Page 107. Jan Taylor typeset and laid out the book and provided the postcard on the first page. Mike Egeler provided the cover graphics.

All the photos were provided by the U.S. Forest Service except where noted:

PHPC	Pictorial Histories Publishing Company
HWP	Historic Wallace Preservation Society, Harry English Collection
OHS	Oregon Historical Society
UI	University of Idaho
DS	Dave Strohmaier
LRD	Lochsa Ranger District

Table of Contents

September 15, 1910

Forest Supervisors:

I think it is worth while to bring to your attention the following extract from the speech of Theodore Roosevelt at Pueblo. I will be glad to have you bring this to the attention of your Rangers.

"I want to call your attention to the wonderful work done by the Forest Service in fighting the great forest fires this year. With the very inadequate appropriation made for the Forest Service, nevertheless that service, because of the absolute honesty and efficiency with which it has been conducted, has borne itself so as to make an American proud of having such a body of public servants: and they have shown the same qualities of heroism in battling with the fire, at the peril and sometimes to the loss of their lives, that the firemen of the great cities show in dealing with burning buildings."

Very truly yours,

W.B. Greeley
District Forester

Forest fires have raged over the United States for centuries. One of the most destructive occurred in Wisconsin in 1871. More than 1,280,000 acres burned and 1,182 lives were lost. AMERICAN RED CROSS

The Beginning

By 1910 the nation had made significant progress in its movement away from "frontier freebooting," a philosophy which had lead to the reckless and wholesale exploitation of natural resources, including America's forests. In 1891 Congress had authorized the withdrawal of forest reserves from the public domain, and in 1897 legislation had insured the proper care, protection, and management of the public forests. Authorization for employing "guardians" of the forests had been granted; in addition, the reserves had been opened for regulated use only. A start had been made in directing the nation toward a policy of wise use and conservation of resources.

In 1898 Gifford Pinchot had been appointed first chief of the Division of Forestry of the Department of the Interior, the forerunner of the Forest Service. Pinchot was the nation's first native professional forester, experienced in managing a large private forest in North Carolina and personally familiar with many of the new forest reserves. In 1905 Congress transferred the forest reserves to the Department of Agriculture, and the Bureau of Forestry became known as the Forest Service.

An office for District One of the Forest Service, which administered timberlands stretching from parts of Michigan to northeastern Washington, was set up in Missoula, Montana, in 1908. District Forester William B. Greeley and his assistant F.A. Silcox were hard put as to how they could most effectively use their meagre manpower; each man in the service was responsible for 250,000 to 400,000 acres. Early day forest rangers, riding horseback over mountain trails, were primarily custodians of the forests, protecting them from fire, game poachers, timber and grazing trespassers, and exploiters of various sorts.

Not only undermanned but also underequipped, the national forests were lacking in lookout points, trails, telephone lines, pack trails, tools, and tool caches, especially in the heavily timbered areas of western Montana and northern Idaho. Nor were the private forest industries or railroads particularly prepared to develop significant fire protection or fire fighting measures.

The Forest Service had finally been able to set up a basic organization for combating forest fires in early 1910. It looked like a plan might be needed, for ominous signs presaged debilitating fires.

The moisture situation was a dramatic departure from normal, average precipitation in the northern Rocky Mountains being ten to twenty inches annually in valleys and forty to sixty inches locally in many of the mountainous areas.

In 1909 some parts of neighboring Washington state reported precipitation to be the lowest in forty years. As early as March 1910, abnormally low amounts of moisture and soaring, high temperatures were recorded. In Montana and Idaho, temperatures for the month of April were the highest on record, and no relief was in sight by the time May rolled around.

In June the statistics were becoming even more frightening. The annual precipitation in District One was averaging only one–half inch, and most weather stations in the area reported no rain in July.

By August the United States Weather Bureau was classifying the area as being in a state of unprecedented drought, with streams measuring record lows. Sluggish rivers and creeks ran low and tepid; trout fought for the few remaining shady, deep pools. Brown–edged, dull, brittle pine needles and parched underbrush covered forest floors. Territorial patterns for wildlife changed as watering places dried up or had to be bypassed because of algae and stagnant, brackish water. Even loggers on the normally cool "hoot owl" shift found the air stifling, the trees that they felled dry, and the skid roads hot and dusty.

What appeared to be welcome rain clouds frequently welled up in the skies to the west, and they dryly scudded on east, marking up still more frustrating, rainless days for the parched Northwest.

Clarence B. Swim of the Forest service declared:

The late summer of 1910 approached with ominous, sinister, and threatening portents. Dire catastrophe seemed to permeate the very atmosphere. Through the first weeks of August, the sun rose a coppery red ball and passed overhead red and threatening as if announcing an impending disaster. This fiery red sun continued day after day. The air felt close, oppressive and explosive. Drift smoke clouded the sky day after day.

August was an anomaly. While precipitation was dangerously down, temperatures had dropped to unseasonable lows. In some places in Montana mean temperatures were ten degrees below average. The Weather Bureau claimed that the phenomenon was caused by smoke in the atmosphere.

In an effort to induce the much–needed rain, dynamite was exploded at Wallace, Idaho. The theory was that thunder and lightning caused rain; therefore, "manufactured thunder and lightning should also bring precipitation. The *Missoulian* of August 17 reported that dynamite had been exploded spasmodically in the town for sixty hours, with only one shower of rain falling.

The entire weather situation startled the fledgling Forest Service. They had hoped for cool, wet weather to help make the job of setting up a basic fire fighting organization in the twenty–two national forests of District One less overpowering. There was to be no such reprieve.

The Supervisor's Office at Wallace in 1908, three years after the Forest Service was established and two years before the great fire, which would surely test the will and stamina of these workers.

Bull River Ranger Station in the Cabinet National Forest, ten miles from Noxon, Montana, in 1908.

Interior of the Lolo National Forest office in the Hammond Block, Missoula, Montana. PHPC

U.S. Forest Service Officials, District One, 1910

Gifford Pinchot was a member of the National Forest Commission in 1896, chief of the Division of Forestry in 1898, and first chief of the U.S. Forest Service from 1905 to 1910. He graduated from Yale University in 1889 and was a leading figure in the conservation movement during the early part of the twentieth century.

W.B. Greeley was chief forester of District One from 1908 to 1911. His domain covered eastern Washington, northern Idaho, Montana and western South Dakota. He later became chief of the U.S. Forest Service.

F.A. Silcox served as assistant chief forester of District One in 1910. He became chief of the U.S. Forest Service in 1933.

Elers Koch was supervisor of the Lolo National Forest in 1910. He was a graduate of Yale University and worked for the Forest Service in many positions for 40 years until his retirement in 1944.

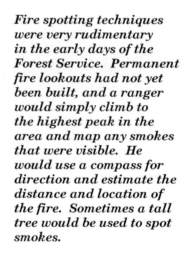

Fire spotting techniques were very rudimentary in the early days of the Forest Service. Permanent fire lookouts had not yet been built, and a ranger would simply climb to the highest peak in the area and map any smokes that were visible. He would use a compass for direction and estimate the distance and location of the fire. Sometimes a tall tree would be used to spot smokes.

Putting up first leg of a ladder on a stripped tree. Alternate ranger is in the crow's nest, lookout fireman is on the ground. LRD

The map board was used to "sight in" fires after locating them from the crow's nest. LRD

East Dennis Lookout LRD

FOREST FIRES!

The great annual destruction of forests by fire is an injury to all persons and industries. The welfare of every community is dependent upon a cheap and plentiful supply of timber, and a forest cover is the most effective means of preventing floods and maintaining a regular flow of streams used for irrigation and other useful purposes.

To prevent forest fires Congress passed the law approved May 5, 1900, which—

Forbids setting fire to the woods, and
Forbids leaving any fires unextinguished.

This law, for offenses against which officers of the FOREST SERVICE can arrest without warrant, provides as maximum punishment—

A fine of $5,000, or imprisonment for two years, or both, if a fire is set maliciously, and

A fine of $1,000, or imprisonment for one year, or both, if fire results from carelessness.

It also provides that the money from such fines shall be paid to the school fund of the county in which the offense is committed.

THE EXERCISE OF CARE WITH SMALL FIRES IS THE BEST PREVENTIVE OF LARGE ONES. Therefore all persons are requested—

1. Not to drop matches or burning tobacco where there is inflammable material.

2. Not to build larger camp fires than are necessary.

3. Not to build fires in leaves, rotten wood, or other places where they are likely to spread.

4. In windy weather and in dangerous places, to dig holes or clear the ground to confine camp fires.

5. To extinguish all fires completely before leaving them, even for a short absence.

6. Not to build fires against large or hollow logs, where it is difficult to extinguish them.

7. Not to build fires to clear land without informing the nearest officer of the FOREST SERVICE, so that he may assist in controlling them.

This notice is posted for your benefit and the good of every resident of the region. You are requested to cooperate in preventing its removal or defacement, which acts are punishable by law.

JAMES WILSON,
Secretary of Agriculture.

U.S. FOREST SERVICE, DARBY RANGER DISTRICT

The Fires

The first forest fire of the 1910 season began in the Blackfoot National Forest of northwestern Montana on April 29. In rapid–fire succession several other burns charred District One. Privately, forest supervisors were told to gird up for a nasty fire season and to purchase the necessary fire fighting equipment. If District One Forester William Greeley was disturbed by the fires, he did not make his feelings public. In early June he claimed that fire danger would be reduced and he looked forward to the best yet for the five–year old Forest Service.

By late June fires were burning in all the forests of the district, most of them in northern *Idaho* and western Montana. During the first two weeks of July, new fires sprang up almost daily. Some of them were contained, but many were not. By mid–July it was clear that the forest fire situation was the most dangerous since 1889.

While most Forest Service jurisdictional boundaries of its almost twenty–six million acres in the district were clear, a few key ones were not. Glacier National Park, for instance, had been created by Congress on May 11, 1910. No money had been appropriated for protecting the park from fires. Nonetheless, when serious fires broke out in the park during mid–July, District Forester Greeley dispatched fire fighters from the neighboring Flathead and Blackfeet National Forests to prevent park fires from spreading into the two forests. Greeley stated in the July 17, 1910 *Missoulian*:

We could not wait to make the necessary inquiries from Washington—the situation was too serious— so we sent men from the two forests mentioned to fight the park fires; the matter of meeting the expenses will be settled afterward.

A number of matters had to be decided afterward. There wasn't sufficient time to settle them at the moment, nor was there time to wait for the bureaucracy to act.

One of the more pressing problems was the lack of manpower. By mid–July, $6,000 had been spent in one week on fire fighters' wages in the Coeur d'Alene National Forest alone. Many of the men were paid on the job by special "disbursing agents" who were ordered to the scene. It was soon decided that instead of paying fire fighters to meet specific emergencies and then release them, it was better to hire as many temporary men as possible and keep them on the payroll to meet future needs. Almost overnight the number of men working for the Forest Service soared to the largest in the history of the agency. Not all fire fighters were paid by the Forest Service. Railroad, mining and lumber companies and protective associations also supplied large numbers of men for the task.

How could the Forest Service, with distric offices in Montana, keep track of the fires and fire fighters? Generally they could not.

The worst fires straddled the Continental Divide between Idaho and Montana in the Coeur d'Alene and Lolo National Forests, along the Bitterroot Range, where fires were breaking out at a rate of three to four per day. The situation was bad, but it was going to get worse.

Primitive transportation, lack of communication and fire fighting equipment, rugged terrain, inadequate numbers of experienced fire fighters and supervisors, and tinderbox conditions in the forests were only some of the problems that plagued effective fire fighting. If these handicaps weren't enough, reports reached the press that some of the ragged, tattered "temporaries" were setting fires themselves to help insure their continuing employment. By today's wage standards, 25 cents per hour may seem poor, but for 1910 it was a good wage. Many of the temporaries were hired at Spokane, Missoula, and Butte where they had been on unemployment roles for long periods of time. Some were drifters, ex–convicts, escaped prisoners, or vagrants. As Chief Greeley put it,

It was a case of hiring anyone we could get. We cleaned out Skid Road in Spokane and Butte. A lot of the temporaries were bums and hoboes. In a bad fire year the temporary is the weakest link in the chain . . . they loafed on the job; some of them quit on the job, but we did have splendid crews from the logging camps and wonderful assistance from Butte miners.

Equipment for the temporaries had to be bought from local stores. Axes, shovels, saws, mattocks, tubs, coffee pots, frying pans, blankets—all sold like proverbial hotcakes. Soon the items were gone from store shelves. Adequate food supplies became a problem, but men who were fighting fires had to be supplied, for over three thousand small fires and ninety major conflagrations were burning in July. Many fires simply were ignored. Although the building of fire lines or the starting of backfires sometimes halted or retarded the devastation of the forests, many fires nevertheless roared and crackled and popped and devoured thousands of acres of the West's finest trees.

It is somewhat surprising, therefore, that on the last day of July, Supervisor Greeley told the news media, "We are holding our own against all the fires within the jurisdiction of [the] district." Greeley's words had hardly been uttered, however, when both the Lolo and Coeur d'Alene forest fires erupted anew during the first week of August.

Within roughly 100 miles of Missoula (generally north and west) fires broke out, encompassing parts of the Rock Creek and Greenough areas, the Seeley Lake and Glacier Park regions, and the Arlee and Dixon areas of the Flathead Indian Reservation. The region west of Missoula, the areas around Taft, Paradise, and St. Regis in Montana and the Grand Forks area of Idaho were among the real and potential victims of forest fires. Fires that were miles in length burned on the Montana—Idaho border. Fires erupted in the Bitterroot Valley south of Missoula.

Charges were leveled against some landowners who lived in an area infested by spotted–fever ticks. They had allegedly set fire to underbrush and timber, hoping to clear out the wood ticks.

The manpower pool was running dangerously low. Not only were additional men needed to fight fires as they sprang up, but replacements were needed to spell the exhausted,

FOREST FIRES

Having put 75 per cent of this county into forest reserves it would seem that the government should be under some obligation to protect the forests from the ravages of fire. There are numerous settlers within the reserves as quite a few homesteads were taken before the forest reserves were created, and being practically surrounded by the government forests the settlers are at the mercy of the fires which find unlimited fuel in the wilderness in which they are obliged to live.

For more than a month settlers, including women and children, have been fighting to save their homes and in nearly every instance the fires have originated on the government lands. The fire which started several weeks ago about twenty miles northwest of Kalispell on the foothill called Pilot Knob, is still burning and from this fire several others have been started by burning brands carried a mile or more by the winds. The settlers living along the eastern line of the reserve at this point have been fighting fire both on their own claims and on the government lands. A few men have been sent out by the government forester to fight the fires but they have refused to assist in controlling the fire on any land not owned by the government, the man in charge of the work for the government saying that settlers would have to take care of the fires on their own claims. This is a very short-sighted policy as a danger to one is a danger to all, but it is directly in line with the weak and inefficient management of the whole fire situation on the government timber reserves. Instead of sending men enough to cope with the situation and keeping them to patrol the fire after it is under control, a few men are sent and at the first moment the fire is under control the men are laid off in order to save expense. After the rain early in July all of the extra men in the government employ were discharged and in about a week the fires were again burning fiercely. If the forces had been kept at work after the rain all of the fires could have been kept under control.

If this part of the country is to be held by the government as an undeveloped wilderness it should at least be so managed as not to endanger the lives and property of the settlers who reside here.

Kalispell Bee
Aug. 2

Co-Operating Against Fires

UNDER an arrangement entered into between the department of agriculture at Washington and the Northern Pacific and Great Northern railways, there should be a decided decrease in the number of fires which are caused by sparks from locomotives along the lines of those roads in the northwest. The agreement was signed by Secretary Wilson for the forest service, and is primarily designed to prevent damage to the national forests from fires along all lines operated by the railroad companies named.

The agreements have in view both the reduction to the lowest point of fire risk from the operation of the railroads and joint action by the forest service and the railroads to fight all fires which may start along the lines. The companies agree to clear and keep clear of inflammable material a strip of varying width, as conditions may demand, up to 200 feet beyond the right of way and to provide all engines with suitable spark arresters and other standard equipment to prevent the dropping of fire.

It is also stipulated that every effort will be made by the companies to operate their locomotives so as not to cause fires. The protective strip is to be stipulated jointly by representatives of the railroad and the forest service.

Helena Record   *May 6*

LOSES HIS LIFE IN FOREST FIRE

Missoula, Aug. 2.—William Hovey olleys, youngest member of the Polleys Lumber company of Lincoln, Nebraska, and this city, was killed today in the woods near Tammany, a station on the Coeur d'Alene branch of the Northern Pacific, by a falling tree. He was leading a crew of fire fighters and his is the first life to be lost to the forest fires that are scourging western Montana. He died on a train that was bringing him to Missoula.

Today in western Montana, and Idaho, the forest fire situation has assumed the most serious aspect since the first fire some 60 days ago. The forest officials of district No. 1, with headquarters here, are almost overwhelmed with the reports of new fires, old fires spreading, and the cries for help from the rangers and the men in the field attempting to hold the flames in check. The service here echoes the cry for help by calling for men, a young army being needed and the most encouraging thing today is the response to the call, which has been active, and large crews have been gotten together and dispatched to the most serious blazes. More are needed and more are coming—some from Spokane and points west, but more from Butte and Montana towns. Supervisor White of the Bitter Root forest arrived with 90 men this morning from Butte, and took them up the valley to be used in his district. About 25 more men have been secured in Butte and will arrive later today. They will be sent west into the Coeur d'Alene district by a special Northern PPacific train and distributed at several points along the route from where they will be taken into the field.

FORESTS IN PARK ABLAZE!

BY ASSOCIATED PRESS.

Washington, Aug. 15.—The fury of the forest fires in the Glacier National park in Montana has not abated, according to the latest reports received here by the interior department. Major William R. Logan, supervisor of the new park, in a telegram received by Acting Secretary of the Interior Pierce today made another appeal that troops be rushed to his assistance. It is assumed, however, that the dispatch was sent before Major Logan received word that soldiers were en route.

Major Logan was instructed to communicate with the commander of Fort Wright at Spokane, who would inform him how many soldiers had been placed at his disposal and when they would arrive. If the number prove inadequate, more will be sent.

Butte Intermountain
Aug. 15

Regular Soldiers Now Aiding in Fight Against Fires in Forests of Western Montana

(Special Dispatch to the Miner.)

Missoula, Aug. 13.—At a conference this morning between Maj. Fred Morgan, superintendent of the Flathead Indian reservation, and W. B. Greeley, forester of district No. 1, the United States troops that arrived today were apportioned between the reservation and the forest service. Two full companies go to the reservation and are now at work, being sent to Arlee. The third company was sent to Packers Meadows, where a base will be established, from which the fight against the fires across the Idaho line will be fought, as soon as the Packers Meadows proposition is in hand.

The fire at the Monitor mine has broken out of control, and is burning fiercely. The situation at Clinton is not as acute as was thought yesterday, and the fire can probably be kept in check. A fire in Belmout creek, in the Blackfoot valley, is in dangerous shape, and hundreds of range horses are being driven to the valley and are crowding the county highways. This blaze is about 20 miles from Bonner, in the direction of the Clearwater country.

Twenty-one additional fire fighters were dispatched to Miller creek today, where the situation is serious. Fires covering from 200 to 300 acres are reported from upper Priest lake, in the Kaniksu forest. The Clearwater forest continues to be a thorn in the flesh of the officials. This district No. 1. Two townships, in an inaccessible portion of the forest are reported to be burning, and little can be done just now to stop the conflagration. One of the men of Supervisor Fren attempted to cross the line into Idaho, but was repelled by surging flames at every point. Arrangements are being made for the sending of more pack trains into the Clearwater country.

Washington, Aug. 13.—Forest fires in the northwest threatening destruction to human life and millions of dollars worth of property, have alarmed officials of the interior department and of the forest service. In response to appeals from the fire zones, additional United States soldiers are being rushed to the scenes to assist in combatting the flames. The soldiers have been despatched to Coeur d'Alene, Idaho, Lewis and Clark, Montana, Wallowa, Ore., and Colville, Wash., national forests, the Flathead Indian reservation, Montana, and the Glacier national park, Montana.

The troops have been spread over the entire fire belt and General Leonard Wood, chief of staff of the army, has informed the interior department that the assistance of the army will be given in meeting the emergency to the limit of the number of soldiers available.

Butte Miner Aug. 14

DUTY OF EVERYONE TO PREVENT FIRES

In discussing the financial side of the forest fire question with particular reference to the general carelessness exercised by campers and even ranchers living within the forests or adjacent thereto, a forestry official said today:

"In the Pacific northwest during the past few years more than $100,000,000 has been spent in the development of the lumber industry and the people of the whole country share the benefits derived from such an expenditure. Burned timber pays no wages and every one should help protect the forests from catching on fire. Not only is the burned timber useless but the denuded mountains injure the surrounding country and agricultural valleys by the loss of moisture which always follows forest destruction. This year's reports and the present conditions in this and other sections of the United States help emphasize the necessity of caution and adequate fire protection. Although no wide spread disaster has overtaken any one community, still the actual loss by fire has been enormous and will be burdensome. The potential loss—destruction of young growth and sweeping away of forest covers on cut-over land—is even greater and the problem when viewed from this standpoint is serious and demands more serious thought from those inclined to pass it over too lightly. Caution about fires in the woods can not be too strongly observed."

Missoula Herald
Aug. 1

Ft. Benton Press Aug. 17

TO CHECK FOREST FIRES.

Dynamite Exploded For Purpose of Causing Rain.

WALLACE, Idaho, Aug. 15.—Two companies of infantry from Fort George Wright, Spokane, arrived here early today to aid in quenching the great forest fire in the Coeur d'Alene national forest reserve. Conditions continue to improve. Dynamite was exploded in Wallace yesterday with the hope of bringing rain and a small shower fell during the night.

A ten-mile trench has been dug around the Big creek fire and it is believed that only a heavy wind will cause it to get away from the fire fighters.

A large crew of men on the Borax fire on Idaho mountain went on a strike yesterday because they believed the foreman was not a union sympathizer. Men were sent out today to take their places.

WASHINGTON, Aug. 15.—The fury of the forest fires in the Glacier national park in Montana has not abated, according to the latest reports received here by the interior department. Major Wm. R. Logan, supervisor of the new park, in a telegram received by Acting Secretary of the Interior Pierce today, made another appeal that troops be rushed to his assistance. It is assumed, however, that the dispatch was sent before Major Logan received word that soldiers were enroute.

Major Logan was instructed to communicate with the commander of Fort Wright at Spokane, Wash., who would inform him how many soldiers had been placed at his disposal and when they would arrive. If the force proves inadequate, more will be sent.

Forest Ranger Brackett, who has his headquarters at the Geo. Voorheis ranch, arrested a man named Harry Gibford Wednesday morning for leaving a camp fire burning on the reserve about two miles above the Elliott ranch. Gibford and his wife had been to Wisdom with a load of vegetables from over in Idaho and had camped there Tuesday night on his return journey. When they broke camp next morning they either neglected or forgot to put out their fire, and Ranger Brackett, who passed that way shortly after they left extinguished the fire and rode after the couple and placed them under arrest. They were taken before Justice of the Peace Woodworth, but as no damage had been done and as it was a first offense, allowed them to go, after a reprimand.

Big Hole
Breezes
Aug. 11

sometimes injured or dead, fire fighters in the forests.

In early August, 100 to 150 men per day were being recruited from places such as Butte, Missoula, and Spokane. By August 5, 1,200 to 1,500 men had been employed to fight fires.

Nervous Forest Service supervisors asked President Taft to send United States troops to help fight the fires, and on August 8, Taft ordered troops to stand by. They would be released on demand to the Forest Service for fire fighting duty. Troops at Fort Missoula and Fort William Henry Harrison in Helena were expected to help, but at the time they were on annual maneuvers in Washington state.

Wallace, Idaho, was the most threatened settlement in the Coeur d'Alene National Forest, and possibly in all of the forests. William G. Weigle, Coeur d'Alene National Forest Supervisor, ordered two companies of United States soldiers from Fort George Wright (Spokane), Washington, on August 13. They arrived in Wallace the following day. Two days later, 100 blacks of the 25th Infantry from Fort Missoula, commanded by white officers, arrived in Wallace. Some troops were sent to fight fires; others were assigned a waiting game until they heard from Weigle. Temporarily at least, Wallace seemed out of imminent danger.

But the same could not be said for most of the forests which suffered devastating fire damage between August 10 and 20. Reports filtered in from the Clearwater, Lolo, Cabinet, Flathead, Blackfeet, and Kaniksu National Forests that fires were racing along faster than a man could walk. Civilian fire fighters and the

Scene in the St. Joe National Forest before the great fire of 1910. The Chicago, Milwaukee & Puget Sound (later known as the Milwaukee Road) had cut its right–of–way through the forest in 1907-08. PHPC

military worked together to control the fires, and as August 20 neared, it seemed that simple techniques such as backfires, trenches, and pinching flames into less valuable timber stands were bringing hard–fought victory. It looked like Supervisor Greeley's statement of August 17 might be true—that only an exceptional wind could truly endanger the area.

As it happened, the wind that started on the afternoon of August 20, 1910, was exceptional. A gale of hurricane force swept through most of the national forests of northern Idaho and western Montana. The hardest hit areas were in the Clearwater and Coeur d'Alene National Forests of Idaho and the Lolo and Cabinet National Forests of Montana. Although fires had been burning on several Forest Service lands and on some private land, what came be called the "big blowup" basically started in the Nez Perce National Forest near Elk City, Idaho. It then scampered across the Clearwater National Forest and continued through the Bitterroot Range into western Montana. This was a wind–fed fire— a wild, surging, fierce, screaming, unrelenting, furnace–like fire that lapped up trees and wildlife and buildings and men. The heat of the fire and the great masses of flaming gas created powerful whirlwinds that mowed down trees in advance of the flames and fed oxygen to the fires, which swept thirty to fifty miles wide across mountain ranges and even rivers. There was no stopping it— the fire was a killer that could not be fought, only avoided at best. As ranger John S. Baird described the fire fighting situation, "We honestly

did our best, but it was not good enough on that fire."

The wind of the blazing demon roared and blew with such force that it threatened to topple seasoned riders from their horses; it howled and screamed and downed mammoth trees. The heat was unbelievably intense. As the red mass boiled and swirled, snapped and snarled dragon–like, it swooped down on ranger Ed Thenon's crew of thirty men on Moose Creek in the Selway National Forest on August 20. About ten o'clock that night the sky was aglow with a pink color spread across a width of several miles—in strange contrast to the pitch dark it had been in the afternoon when the crew had set up camp for the night.

Thenon was awakened by pine needles and debris falling on his tent, but it wasn't until Louis Fitting mistakenly thought he saw a falling star begin a fire across the creek from the camp that Thenon ordered his men to move the supplies to a sand strip on Moose Creek. They couldn't overrun the fire, so Thenon ordered his crew to get in the creek, lie down and put wet blankets over their heads. Two of the men were driven senseless from fear. The cook became violently insane and was forced by three men to lie in the creek. Thenon wrote that the second man was "dancing around and singing a lullaby," and that although a wet blanket was thrown over the man's head, he wouldn't lie down. Nevertheless, the crew somehow managed to survive as the crown fire passed over them—a red, breathtaking monster. Thenon later wrote that he stuck his head in a bucket to escape the heat and thus saved his life. The unfortunate "lullaby boy," as Thenon called him, did not regain his rationality, and had to be institutionalized.

One of the crew was a near casualty. He had gone to the creek for water and was almost killed by a falling tree that had been charred in the fire. Lou Fitting's brother Ray had left camp earlier to scout the fire situation in the North Fork of Moose Creek. When the fire hit, he took refuge in Moose Creek under an overhanging ledge. By keeping under his coat in the creek, he managed to survive. As dead fish began to float by him, however, he wondered—if the water was hot enough to kill the fish, would he be boiled alive? It was indeed fortunate that no lives were lost in the Clearwater Forest.

Although the Pend Oreille National Forest was not burned as extensively as many, several fires broke out in the region. Most fires occurred near the towns of Clark Fork and Cabinet, Idaho. It was in one of three forests in District One where fire fighters lost their lives.

A relatively small fire was burning in DeFaut Gulch, a small, dry ravine near Cabinet, Idaho. W.E. LaMonte and his crew of ten men worked hard, and they managed to bring the fire under control. The exhausted crew was camped about one mile from the fire line in a two to three acre clearing. As the big burn rushed along to rekindle the fire, William T. Brashear, a forest guard in charge of the area, ordered the men to soak their clothes and bedding in water and to place their blankets over their heads and lie down near the spring in the middle of the clearing. Two men, J. Plant and J. Harris, dazed or demented, threw off their bedding, rushed into the fire, and burned to death only a few yards from where the rest of the terrified crew lay.

Forester Edward G. Stahl wrote that the flames were hundreds of feet high, "fanned by a tornadic wind so violent that the flames flattened out ahead, swooping to earth in great darting curves, truly a veritable red demon from hell."

Four men were killed in the Cabinet National Forest, all in the Swamp Creek fire. Much of the damage occurred in the Clark Fork Valley, where homesteads, towns, and sawmills were destroyed. The railroad station at Tuscor burned, and a sawmill at Trout Creek was obliterated along with 13 million feet of white pine lumber and horses and pigs.

Although H.S. Kaufman was the forest ranger in charge of the area, Roy Engle of Noxon, Montana, was directly in charge of a crew of about twenty–five men working on what was known as the Swamp Creek division of the Tuscor fire. On August 21, Engle's group was working along Swamp Creek about one dozen miles from its mouth. Kaufman was working with a crew along the Clark Fork at the mouth of Swamp Creek. Kaufman ordered Engle to bring his men out of the area, for they were in danger of being trapped by the raging inferno. As the fire closed in on them, Engle headed up Swamp Creek to a large body of slide rock. They stopped on the denuded hillside, digging holes in the rock for further protection.

The fire swept up the gulch and side hill, a top fire consuming everything in its path and throwing burning brands among the men. Five men on the verge of dementia panicked and clambered wildly over the slide rock and up the mountain. The fifth man in the escape group saw that the others were doomed and hurriedly tumbled back to the slide rock area, burned severely but not fatally. The Forest Service report stated,

The other four men perished when been charred in the fire the fire struck them. Several other members of the crew were more or less burned, and all of them were nearly blind from smoke and heat.

The names of fire fighters George Strong, George Fease, E. Williams, and A.G. Bourette were added to the fatality list. This incident occurred about midnight on August 20.

The Coeur d'Alene National Forest lost more timber and human lives than any other area in District One. It also had more towns and fire fighters than any other forest. And it had a folk hero—Edward C. Pulaski, descendent of Polish Count Casimir Pulaski, a hero of the American Revolutionary War.

Pulaski knew the country well, having prospected much of the area for nearly a quarter of a century. The forty–year–old Pole was in charge of about of about 150 men in the Big Creek area of the St. Joe and Big Creek branches of the Coeur d'Alene River. When the hurricane struck, Pulaski was checking on his crews on Placer Creek, southwest of Wallace, Idaho. Pulaski was going to lead a crew of about forty men toward Wallace, about ten miles away.

About midway through the trip, Pulaski realized that fires had

Edward C. Pulaski was born in 1868 and left his Green Springs, Ohio, home in 1884 to head west. He landed in Mullan, Idaho, but soon headed for Butte, Montana, where he worked in the mines and the woods. In 1908 he joined the fledgling U.S. Forest Service in the Coeur d'Alene National Forest. He spent many years with the Service and died in 1931.

stopped the crew's progress. Although some of the men began to panic, Pulaski assured them that they would be safe. As they headed for the shelter of two mines located ahead, fire was rapidly lapping at their rear. Pulaski inspected the tunnels to determine their relative safety. The tunnel of the War Eagle mine seemed best, perhaps because it was the larger of the two. Forty–three men and two horses headed to-

View of the mouth of the War Eagle mine tunnel on Placer Creek in which Ranger Edward Pulaski and his crew of over 40 men took refuge from the fire on August 20. Five men and two horses died in the tunnel that night. Some of the fire fighters' clothes, a saddle and stirrup were still at the site a few weeks after the disaster.

Seven fire fighters were burned alive when they crowded into the homesteader's root cellar at the bottom of the photograph at Beauchamp's homestead on the St. Joe National Forest.

ward the War Eagle, and forty–two men and two horses reached the safety of the tunnel before the fires struck them.

One man had chosen to run. The *Daily Idaho Press* of Wallace reported in its August 22 issue:

Three of the rescue party walked over to where the man lay on the trail, supposing the body to be a burned log. On the return all recognized the body for what it was.

Pulaski ordered the men to lie down with their faces on the tunnel floor, while he hung blankets over the tunnel entrance. He continued to throw water on the blankets and nearby timbers until he fainted. Somehow the laws of physics worked against the crew, for the cool air was sucked from the tunnel, and the heat and smoke were forced in. Everyone lost consciousness at least some time during the ordeal. One man recovered and scrambled the five miles or so to Wallace for help. He arrived about 3 AM, August 21. A rescue party was hurriedly assembled and sped to the tunnel. The men were dragged from it, and five were found dead from suffocation. The rest of the crew, including Pulaski, ultimately recovered.

Almost three years later, the Sunday *Star* of Washington, D.C., (July 20, 1913) was singing the praises of Pulaski, claiming he had withstood an emergency "such as sear the souls of lesser men."

While Pulaski and his crew had suffered through a hell–on–earth nightmare at the War Eagle tunnel, ranger John Bell's crew had scurried to the clearing on Joseph Beau-champ's homestead on the Middle Fork of Big Creek. The clearing had a small stream running through it, and Bell and his crew of fifty or so crammed into the shallow stream and laid face down in it. Seven of the men hid in a small storage cave which Beauchamp had dug. First came the violent windstorm which snapped off nearly all the trees in the area. The crown fire followed with heat so scorching that the men in the creek had the skin on the back of their necks and the hair on the back of their heads burned off. A tree fell on three men, killing them, while the seven in the cave burned to death.

The "cave" may have only been a prospect hole five feet in length, ,according to the *Daily Idaho Press* of Wallace on August 23. The newspaper declared, "The men were burned to such a crisp that they could not be removed from the tunnel prospect hole, so they were buried there, dirt being thrown over hole."

That same issue of the *Daily Idaho Press* carried yet another description of the grisly scene at the Big Creek fire.

The survivors were startled to see a person in human form, but who resembled a ghost more than anything else, suddenly fall over a log and crawl under another. His clothing had been mostly burned off and his body was fearfully burned. He was raving when the other men rescued him and it was necessary to drag him from underneath the log. He breathed his last soon after being carried to water.

The *Press* reported thirteen dead from the fire, three more than Elers

Koch in his *History of the Forest Fires in Idaho and Western Montana*.

Six hours after Wallace citizens had been notified of the fate of the Pulaski crew, a survivor of the Bell crew notified residents that yet another team of men was in danger. It took the Wallace rescuers two full days and nights to open a trail to the injured crew twelve miles from Wallace. The ten men were buried at Beauchamp's clearing. The balance of Bell's crew was hospitalized at Wallace. They all recovered.

Still another crew was trapped in the hurricane of August 20. Twenty–five–year–old ranger William R. Rock with about seventy men were on Setzer Creek, about six miles northeast of Avery, Idaho. Rock first tried to head toward Avery but was cut off by fires. He turned, instead, toward an area that had burned the previous day. But the rather spectacular nature of the smoke and flames which sometimes shot thousands of feet into the air led to the death of crew member Oscar Weigert who was so frightened by the phenomenon that he apparently thought death preferable to suspense and certain torture. Deserting the crew, he shot himself with a pistol. He was the only casualty in the Rock crew.

Near Avery, Setzer Creek was the setting for yet another horror. Ranger R.N. Debitt, who was in charge of the Avery District, sent a deputy sheriff on the night of August 20 to warn a seventy–man crew to skedaddle for Avery. Most of the men heeded the command, but twenty–eight of them decided that both Debitt and the deputy were exaggerating the situation, so they decided to stay in the forest. No one lived to tell of or write about what happened. All twenty–eight were burned beyond recognition within hours after they had been ordered from the woods. They were found at the extreme head of Storm Creek, the next drainage west of Setzer Creek. Rescuers wrapped the bodies in blankets, sewed the remains in heavy canvas, and buried the men where they had fallen. One of the most dramatic episodes in the big blowup death saga remains a shadowy, eternal mystery.

Lee Hollingshead was a twenty–two–year–old ranger in charge of a sixty man crew on the West Fork of Big Creek. On the evening of August 20, when the men were fighting a fire that was rapidly dancing from Trout Creek, they were surrounded by fire, except for nineteen men who had snaked their way through the torturous fire line to sanctuary on a previously burned over area. Again, panic lead to death as nineteen fire fighters rushed down the hill ahead of the fire to a small cabin where five pack horses were stationed. The structure, known as the Henry Dittman cabin, was surrounded by flames, but the men stayed inside until the roof began burning and falling in on them. They fled from the cabin and tried to break through the onrushing fire line, but the engulfing, mindless, raging fire consumed the bodies of all but one within a few feet from the cabin. The lone survivor managed to wander to the St. Joe River, where a search crew found him. Nearly nude, with the skin on his hands and face burned off, the benumbed fire fighter recovered following a six–week confinement.

Mr. Silcox:-

The telephone line is down between here and Missoula today so I have not been able to get you to inform you of the men reported safe by Friday and Barringer, and did not deem it advisable to send complete list by wire. Friday reports all men and horses safe and provided for. Friday will be in tonight and give details.

Friday's men.
Fred Loth   )
Wm. Ball   )   Guards
Clarence Hunt   )   (at Chamberlain Meadows)
P. S. Friday   )
Dave Cochran   )
J. F. Rumple   )

Additional men.
Arthur Streeter
H. Bovill
James Cameron
H. S. Lawson
H. Wills
J. P. Partridge
J. Bloomhagen
F. W. High
Fred Faus

Barringer got in last night and reports every man and horse safe and also all camp outfits and grub. 15 men are at Amador working on fires at head of Cedar Creek and Trout Creek. Balance of crew are camped at head of Trout Creek working on Trout Creek fire from north.

Barringer's men.
Fred Bland
M. C. Gammell
Alex Ironside
John Lamb
J. D. Chard
Chas. Leon
Thad Pethound

Jack Barnes
Wm. Ronen
C. E. Buss
James Kelleher
Edwards Trail Crew (6 men) (names not known by
        Barringer,- see Koch)
Claffy
Garrison, Clearwater Ranger, and Guards with him and
        about 7 men,- names not known by Barringer.
George Brown
Gilmore Wolan
John Platt
Alfred Britian
Ben Jergins

LaCombe, who had the outfit packing for Haines, returned last night from the Idaho-Montana divide, and reported loss of entire outfit including horses. 11 horses were found dead in one place. No word has come out from Haines or crew yet, but expect something today or tomorrow, and am holding a pack train in readiness to rush in if necessary. Will have all fires in this district lined up by tonight but can not use additional men to work along divide fires for a day or two.

(Signed) F. E. Bonner.

A bill for boarding men on fire crew should give the names and the meals each man received.

When men are hired who are to be paid by the Big Blackfoot Lumber Company under the cooperative agreement, the time should be sent to this office as usual and the time slips will be approved and either the men will be sent to Bonner for their pay or the checks will be mailed to them by the Big Blackfoot Lumber Co.

All fires should be reported on Form 874-6, whether inside or outside of the Forest, provided you did any work in connection with the fire. Please be very careful to fill out the blank in full, especially in regard to the cost of cooperative assistance which can in most cases be secured only from your report. A map should be submitted on the township plat form of all fires of
over
5 acres and over. Do not look reporting small fires extinguished even though no damage was done.

When possible, fires on which extra help is needed should be reported to this office by telephone. If you are unable to get the office by phone do not hesitate to go ahead and hire what men you think are needed to put the fire out. Please keep me in touch with progress as much as possible by letter and telephone. If you need men and are unable to get them locally we are generally able to get plenty in Missoula and can ship them out on the first train. Do not try to fight a big fire with a small crew. It is more expensive in the end. Do not pull off all the men till the fire is absolutely safe.

Remember that patrol must be kept up if possible and do not tie up yourself and all the guards on your district on one fire. As long as you have more than one man to each fire keep some one on patrol.

Very truly yours,

Elers Koch

Forest Supervisor.

Hollingshead returned to the death scene the next day to find the remains of eighteen men, five horses, and a black bear. The blanket and canvas enshrouded remains of the men, none of whom could be identified, were buried where they had perished.

Like Hollingshead, ranger James Danielson was only twenty–two years old that August when the mountains roared. Danielson had a crew of eighteen men on the Stevens Peak fire five miles south of Mullan, Idaho. Danielson led his men to a small clearing in the forest where they burned the beargrass in hope that the fire would not burn the area a second time. But it did.

The men covered their faces with blankets and decided to tough it out in clearing. Although the fire touched the area, the blankets saved the men, who suffered badly burned faces and hands. One man accidentally inhaled the flames and died on the spot. The rest were sent by pack train and by a Northern Pacific special train to Wallace, where they were hospitalized for one to six weeks. Three continued to suffer stiff hands, but the rest fully recovered.

Forty–year–old S.M. Taylor was in charge of fighting the Bullion fire along the Montana–Idaho line east of Wallace. Taylor's crew of about sixty men was surrounded by fire, but he led them to the tunnel of the Bullion Mine. Larry Ryson was one of the fire fighters who assured Taylor that the tunnel would be a safe place to wait out the fire; Ryson himself had helped to build it, and he knew it well. The men, except for eight, penetrated the shaft far enough to pass an overhead air vent.

Smoke poured down the air shaft and suffocated the eight who were nearer the mine entrance; the rest were spared. The dead were buried on the site. About ten days later, when the Northern Pacific's tracks and trestles had been repaired, the bodies were disinterred and brought to the railroad tracks, where a special car took them to Dorsey. The trestle there was still burned out, however, so the bodies were transferred to yet another special train which had been sent from Wallace. The corpses were delivered to the Wallace morgue and prepared for burial. A few days later the remains were buried in the Wallace cemetery.

Deaths were being announced with depressing regularity as the big burn swept the forests. Fire fighters in the Coeur d'Alene forest alone accounted for seventy–two deaths.

For a week or so after the holocausts of August 20 and 21, it seemed that more names would be added to the list of the dead. Ranger Joe B. Halm's crew had been battling fires in the Coeur d'Alene National Forest in the Bean Creek area near the headwaters of the St. Joe River since late July. The fire fighting success had been so good that just before the big blowup Halm had reduced his crew from 85 to 18. When the men saw the fire bearing down on them on the fateful day of August 20, they neared hysteria. Halm ordered the men to stay in camp and sternly punctuated his order with a hand on his holstered revolver. The frightened men sought safety on a gravel bar in the middle of Bean Creek. Despite 60-70 mile–per–hour winds, falling trees, and scorching fire, Halm's crew survived.

They picked their way through the charred, still-warm forests toward Wallace. Six days later they met a messenger from Wallace, part of a search party led by Assistant Forester Roscoe Haines.

It took them one week to claw through the scattered and broken twisted mass of trees and snags that looked something like jackstraws. In some places the debris was five trees deep, but they had managed to survive the big blowup and wend their way out of an immense, blackened death trap that had engulfed many others.

Perhaps, like Edward G. Stahl, a Forest Service employee who walked out of a forest fire in the Cabinet area that same summer, the men thought that the small fires flickering dimly in the darkness high on the blackened snags which they had struggled through could be candles burning for the dead.

The caption on this H. English photo of the Bullion Mine reads: "3 days before the great disaster Aug. 21-10. 10 men lost their lives at this place." HWP

One of the few photos showing the actual fire. A fire line has been built on the extreme right near the Bullion Mine near Wallace, Idaho.

Cooking dinner on the fire line. HWP

Our Experience with The Fires

by Mr. Swaine

For days the air had been laden with smoke, flying embers, ashes, singed twigs and moss—some pieces as large as a hand or foot falling promiscuously about. Needles from the fir and pine trees rained profusely through the air, falling like showers upon roofs and the ground. The sound was identical with that of rain. It was evident that fires were raging in almost every direction and that day by day, they were drawing nearer to us. Our constant prayer was for rain.

It has been said the Divine Providence requires His children to prove every word they utter, and in the thirteen years of my residence in the Coeur d'Alene's it has been a constant boast with me that the wind never blows here; and the frequent, abundant, delightful showers keep everything fresh, lovely and beautiful. But alas! The wind CAN blow in Idaho and weeks can pass without rain as had been proven in the weeks of drought.

In the distance the reflection of the ruddy glow in the sky and the great crimson sun, seeming to stand out like a gigantic, blood–red orange; a perfect sphere at which one could gaze with ease through the smoke, had been a most beautiful and awe–inspiring sight. The mighty roar of the burning forest resembled the sound of a storm at sea, as expressed by those familiar with that sound. The splendor of the scene was transformed into terror on Saturday, August 20, 1910, when the fires were so near that we were forced to realize that our little village was in imminent danger and that a strong wind might at any moment, prove our destroyer. Before three o'clock PM, it became so dark from smoke, we were obliged to turn on the lights. Bats flew about thinking the night had arrived, and indeed it was enough to make anyone batty. The air became hot and oppressive and the reflection of fires all around us made danger feel uncomfortably near. The falling fragments were now veritible brands, many of the great twigs bearing live fire; and all agreed that our worst fears were about to be realized. Groups of men began congregating at street corners discussing the scene and a sort of reverential silence seemed to have settled upon the place. About five o'clock the business houses and streets were given a thorough soaking by means of the fire hose, as had been done each day for weeks. Every dwelling received a similar application with a garden hose and from that moment, it was a constant conflict with a furious enemy for two nights and two days. With the evening came the wind from the south carrying the Red Terror toward us. Telephones became active, people began discussing the situation seriously, and altogether, a spirit of intense alarm supplanted that of awe. Among those mighty mountains which seemed one mass of flames were many precious lives, we knew, firefighters and prospectors, and we wondered how they could possibly escape.

Night came on us with its added darkness. The screeching, fiendish roar of the fire increased. The flames were headed right for us. Wallace, the metropolis of the Coeur d'Alene's, just seven miles west was suffering a worse fate. The town was already on fire, and believing the outlet eastward most accessible, hospital inmates and women and children were hurried by special trains, through Mullan toward Missoula. Many of our frightened inhabitants, mostly women and children, took advantage of these trains and left our stricken town. It was noticeable that the few men who chose to go, were the foreign element employed in the mines, who had nothing to lose but could carry in a suitcase their savings which would eventually drift back to the fatherland regardless of conditions.

Our brave, courageous citizens turned out enmasse and successfully backfired the path of the flames and by three o'clock AM, Sunday morning, danger from that direction seemed over, but half of Wallace had been wiped out, the wind had changed and their fire was traveling this way. As yet, the river was between it and us. Telephone poles had burned as well as part of the railroad track, cutting off all communication aside from what could be ascertained by messengers and horseback.

About five o'clock AM, the wind subsided and danger seeming over for the moment, the worn citizens started home for a few hours' rest when their attention was arrested by an appalling sight. Thirteen burned, blackened, almost charred men, holding their painful hands in the air,

scarcely knowing how or where they were going, yet aiming for one goal, the physician's office, came hastening into town. They were fire-fighters who had been sent out days before, to arrest, if possible, the progress of the fires. All but two succeeded in reaching town, but the agonies of these poor men can only be realized by those who witnessed their writhings and expressions. Two physicians, assisted by willing volunteers, hastily did all that was possible to relieve their suffering. A temporary hospital was prepared in a vacant store building and the wants of the sufferers satisfied as far as circumstances permitted.

By eight o'clock AM, the wind resumed its zeal from the west. The fire jumped the river and was covering the ranges west of us and traveling northward. The heat, smoke and humidity were almost unbearable. Conveyances of every description were pressed into service and women and children hurried across the burned district to special trains west of Wallace waiting to carry refugees to safety. The day was like a horrible night, but through the trying hours was that dread of another even more terrible night to come. All too soon it came and those of us who witnessed it, have termed it the "Night of Terror."

The wind came up with a fury. It seemed to blow in whirls carrying sparks in every direction, but the general trend was northeast. As if by magic, new fires would spring up, here, there and everywhere. In every direction, a mountain of flame faced us. One side of a gulch would be aflame and in an instant the fire would be borne across to the other side, and by leaps and bounds from tree to tree, the terrible destruction continued.

Those familiar with the location of our little village, can, in a measure, picture the scene. Others never can. The mountains so high and steep with the narrow gulches between, resembled curtains of fire suspended from the clouds. Absolute property loss seemed positive but we believed out lives could be saved.

Every emergency reaches a crises; and when the extremity arrives, the last resort is adopted. Consequently, when fires had completely surrounded us, and were crowding within a few feet of our doors, and sparks raining like water, it was unaniamously agreed that the town must surely go unless the entire west, north and east could be protected by backfires. The tops of the mountains in these directions were already a mightly billow of flame showering their sparks and brands upon the town below.

Those familiar with forest fires, know how much faster fires travel up than down a mountain side. Hence a fire started almost against the houses would travel with a fury up the hillsides meeting the surging flames in the timber thus clearing the space passed over and leaving a burned district upon which burning fragments might fall without danger. If backfires take the desired course, all is well; but should they be reversed or misdirected by the wind as is often the case, they are only an added menace. It took courage to start more fires with surrounding country already a sea of fire and the wind a veritible fury, but it was our _only_ chance; so a line of men were stationed just a few feet apart, forming a letter s, from the Morning to the Hunter mills, just a few feet in the rear of the buildings. At the signal each started a blaze.

These fires united in less time that it takes to relate it, and traveled up the mountains, leaping, foaming, rippling over the brush and grass, then bursting into crimson towers as they passed over stately pines and firs. It was a most beautiful sight yet a most terrible one. The mountains south were still on fire. There was now no outlet. Fancy a deep bowl which is completely lined with seething flames, yourself a spectator in the center, and you can in some degree conceive the scene. The screeching, furious howl of the fire, the heat and grandeur withal, was suggestive of the infernal regions, something unreal, unnatural; as our dear, calm Scotch friend who was so unfortunate as to be our guest at that time, expressed as "uncanny." Much of the smoke was carried onward by the high wind. Midnight was as light as day. The mountains never appeared so high is with their blankets of fire and never impressed us as such barriers.

At last the morning dawned. The wind subsided, and with the dawn, our prayers of gratitude went forth. The terror had passed. Not a precious life had been sacrificed, and not a home consumed. It seemed too good to be true. We could scarcely believe it ourselves. We found people asking us and ourselves asking each other how the town had escaped when the fire had passed right over our heads. The reply is as follows: The water supply was unlimited and was most economically and advantageously used; the constant drenching prior to the arrival of the fire and during its presence made things less tangible, but last and best of all was the united, well–managed, thoroughly system atized course pursued by the volunteer fire department and willing citizens, headed and superintended throughout by William Coumerilh, whose council was sought in every instance and whose advice was at no moment disregarded. He seemed to be everywhere at all times with encouragement and assistance for the tireless workers who toiled with him three days and two nights without a moments sleep or rest.

An admirable feature of the entire ordeal, was the calm, stolid reserve which seemed implanted within each soul. With absolute ruin, destruction and poverty, possibly death staring people in their faces, there was no indication of hysteria or a panic at any time.

You will wonder what we were doing all this time. Our guest, Mrs. Swaine, the children and I spent our time serving meals to the firefighters who could not leave their posts except in small relays. However, there came an hour when we bade farewell to the little home, the heat and smoke forcing our departure, and sought a place of safety each with a blanket for protection, quite reconciled to the loss of everything if only our lives might be spared. We took refuge in the schoolhouse—a brick structure situated on a roomy cleared space near the river. This we thought would be the last place to burn although there was danger of suffocation. We remained only about three hours when we returned duly and truly thankful for the tableful of dirty dishes which greeted us, and truly thankful for a sink in which to wash them. We all felt very benevolent after the ordeal and allowed the vagrant livestock, driven as we had been from their homes, to graze unmolested upon our lawns. And we realized as never before, how affliction reduces us to a common level. We had all been united in a single cause, that of saving our all, be it a pocket knife, a home or a fortune. And I echo Mrs. Swaine's remark: "It was a terrible ordeal, but I wouldn't have missed it for anything."

Fire fighters ready to go on the fireline. PHPC

The Big Fire
by Joe Halm

Out of the underbrush dashed a man—grimy, breathless, hat in hand. At his heels came another. Then a whole crew, all casting fearful glances behind them.

"She's coming! The whole country's on fire! Grab your stuff, ranger, and let's get outa here!" gasped the leader.

This scene, on the afternoon of August 20, 1910, stands out vividly in my memory. The place was a tiny, timbered flat along a small creek in the headwaters of the St. Joe River in Idaho. The little flat, cleared of undergrowth to accommodate our small camp, seemed dwarfed beneath the great pines and spruce. The little stream swirled and gurgled beneath the dense growth and windfall, and feebly lent moisture to the thirsting trees along its banks.

For weeks forest rangers with crews of men had been fighting in a vain endeavor to hold in check the numerous fires which threatened the very heart of the great white–pine belt in the forests of Idaho and Montana. For days an ominous, stifling pall of smoke had hung over the valleys and mountains. Crews of men, silent and grim, worked along the encircling fire trenches. Bear, deer, elk and mountain lions stalked stary–eyed and restless through the camps, their fear of man overcome by a greater terror. Birds, bewildered, hopped about in the thickets, their song subdued, choked by the stifling smoke and oppressive heat. No rain had fallen since May. All vegetation stood crisp and brown, seared and withered by the long drought, as if by blight. The

fragrance of summer flowers had given way to the tang of dead smoke. The withered ferns and grasses were covered by a hoar–frost of gray ashes. Men, red–eyed and sore of lung, panted for a breath of untainted air. The sun rose and set beyond the pall of smoke. All nature seemed tense, unnatural and ominous.

It had taken days to slash a way through the miles of tangled wilderness to our fire, sixty–five miles from a railroad. On August 18, this fire was confined within trenches; all seemed well; a day or two more and all would have been considered safe. Difficulties in transportation developed which necessitated reducing our crew from 85 to 18 men.

I had just returned after guiding our remaining packers with their stock to one of our supply camps, when our demoralized crew dashed in. Incoherently, the men told how the fire had sprung up everywhere about them as they worked. The resinous smoke had become darker, the air even more oppressive and quiet. As if by magic, sparks were fanned to flames which licked the trees into one great conflagration. They had dropped their tools and fled for their lives. A great wall of fire was coming out of the northwest. Even at that moment small, charred twigs came sifting out of the ever–darkening sky. The foreman, still carrying his ax, was the last to arrive. "Looks bad," he said. Together we tried to calm the men. The cook hurried the preparation of an early supper. A slight wind now stirred the treetops overhead; a faint, distant roar was wafted to my ears. The men heard it; a sound as of heavy wind, or a distant waterfall. Three men, believing safety lay in flight, refused to stay. "We're not going to stay here and be roasted alive. We're going."

Things looked bad. Drastic steps were necessary. Supper was forgotten. I slipped into my tent and strapped on my gun. As I stepped out a red glow was already lighting the sky. The men were pointing excitedly to the north.

"She's jumped a mile across the canyon," said the foreman, who had been talking quietly to the men. Stepping before them, I carelessly touched the holster of the gun and delivered an ultimatum with outward confidence, which I by no means felt.

"Not a man leaves this camp. We'll stay by this creek and live to tell about it. I'll see you through. Every man hold out some grub, a blanket, and a tool. Chuck the rest in that tent, drop the poles, and bury it."

The men did not hesitate. The supplies, bedding, and equipment were dumped into the tent, the poles jerked out, and sand shoveled over it. Some ran with armloads of canned goods to the small bar in the creek, an open space scarcely thirty feet across. Frying pans, pails, and one blanket for each man were moved there. Meanwhile the wind had risen to hurricane velocity. Fire was now all around us, banners of incandescent flames licked the sky. Showers of large, flaming brands were falling everywhere. The quiet of a few minutes before had become a horrible din. The hissing, roaring flames, the terrific crashing and rending of falling timber was deafening, terrifying. Men rushed back and forth trying to help. One young giant, crazed with

fear, broke and ran. I dashed after him. He came back, wild-eyed, crying, hysterical. The fire had closed in; the heat became intolerable.

All our trust and hope was in the little stream and the friendly gravel bar. Some crept beneath wet blankets, but falling snags drove them out. There was wet air over the water. Armed with buckets, we splashed back and forth in the shallow stream throwing water as high as our strength would permit, drenching the burning trees. A great tree crashed across our bar; one man went down, but came up unhurt. A few yards below, a great log jam, an acre or more in extent, the deposit of a cloudburst in years gone by, became a roaring furnace, a threatening hell. If the wind changed, a single blast from this inferno would wipe us out. Our drenched clothing steamed and smoked; still the men fought. Another giant tree crashed, cutting deep into the bar, blinding and showering us with sparks and spray. But again the men nimbly side-stepped the hideous meteoric monster.

After what seemed hours, the screaming, hissing, and snapping of millions of doomed trees, and the showers of sparks and burning brands grew less. The fire gradually subsided. Words were spoken. The drenched, begrimed men became more hopeful. Some even sought tobacco in their water-soaked clothing. Another hour and we began to feel the chill of the night. The hideous, red glare of the inferno still lighted everything; trees still fell by the thousands. Wearily, the men began to drag the water-soaked blankets from the creek and dry them; some scraped places beneath the fallen trees where they might crawl with their weary, tortured bodies out of reach of the falling snags. The wind subsided. Through that long night beside a man–made fire, guards sat, a wet blanket around their chilled bodies.

Dawn broke almost clear of smoke, the first in weeks. Men began to crawl stiffly out from their burrows and look about. Such a scene! The green, standing forest of yesterday was gone; it its place a charred and smoking mass of melancholy wreckage. The virgin trees, as far as the eye could see, were broken or down, devoid of a single sprig of green. Miles of trees—sturdy, forest giants—were laid prone. Only the smaller trees stood, stripped and broken. The great log jam still burned. Save for the minor burns and injuries, all were safe. nwardly, I gave thanks for being alive. A big fellow, a Swede, the one who had refused to stay, slapped me on the back and handed my gun. I had not missed it.

"You lost her in the creek last night. You save me my life," he said, simply. His lip trembled as he walked away.

The cook had already salvaged a breakfast from the trampled cache in the creek. Frying ham and steaming coffee drove away the last trace of discomfort.

"What are your planes?" asked the foreman, after several cups of coffee.

"First we'll dig out our tent, salvage the grub, and then look the fire over. We'll order more men and equipment and hit the fire again."

Little did I know as I spoke that our fire that morning was but a dot on the blackened map of Idaho and Montana. After breakfast we picked our way through the fire to our camp of yesterday. All was safe. We moved the remaining equipment to the little bar. Our first thought was for the safety of our two packers and the pack stock at our supply camp. The foreman and I set out through the fire over the route of the old trail, now so changed and unnatural. With ever–increasing apprehension we reached the first supply camp where I had left the packers. Only a charred, smoking mass of cans and equipment marked the spot.

What had become the men? Not a sign of life could we find. They must have gone to the next supply camp. We hurried on, unmindful of the choking smoke and our burned shoes. We came upon our last supply camp; this, too, was a charred, smoldering mass. Still no signs of the men. A half mile beyond we suddenly came upon the remains of a pack saddle; then, another; the girths had been cut. Soon we found the blackened remains of a horse. Feverishly we searched farther. Next we found a riding saddle. With a sinking heart we hastened on. More horses and more saddles. The fire was growing hotter. We halted, unable to go farther. We must go back for help and return when the heat had subsided.

Smoke darkened the sky; the wind had risen to a gale; trees were once more falling all about us. We took Shelter in a small cave in a rock ledge where the fire had burned itself out. Here we sat, parched, almost blind with smoke and ashes. Once the foreman voiced my thoughts: "The wind will die down toward night, then we can go back to camp." The fury of the wind, however, increase steadily. Fires roared again, and across the canyon trees fell by the hundreds.

After what seemed like hours, we crept out of our cramped quarters and retraced our steps. The storm had subsided slightly. If the remains of the trail had been littered that morning, it was completely filled now. We came to a bend in the creek where the trail passed over a sharp hogback. As we neared the top, we again came into the full fury of the wind. Unable to stand, pelted by gravel and brands and blinded by ashes, we crawled across the exposed rocky ledges. I had never before, nor have I since, faced such a gale. On the ridges and slopes every tree was now uprooted and down. We passed the grim remains of the horses and supply camps. In the darkness we worked our way back over and under the blackened, fallen trees. Fanned by the wind, the fire still burned fiercely in places. Torn and bleeding, we hurried on, hatless—in the darkness, lighted only by the myriads of fires—I picked the way, the foreman watching for falling trees. While passing along a ledge a great tree tottered above us and went its way to earth, rolling crazily down the slope. We ran for our lives, but the whirling trunk broake and lodged a few feet above. So absorbed were we with our plight that we nearly passed our camp on the little bar in the creek bottom.

By firelight we ate and related our fears as to the fate of the packers. As we talked, one of the men, pointed to the eastern sky, cried, "Look, she's coming again!" The sky in the east had taken on a hideous, reddish glow which became lighter and lighter. To the nerve-racked men it looked like another great fire bearing down upon us. Silently the men watched the phenomenon which lasted perhaps ten minutes. Then the realization came that the sky was clearing of smoke. In another brief space of time the sun shone. Not until then did I know that it was only four o'clock. A change in the wind had shifted the smoke toward the northwest. We later found that the burn extended but a mile or two to the south of us.

Daylight next morning found us chopping and sawing a route back through the now cooled burn toward civilization, searching for our packers. That day I visited a prospector's cabin on a small side creek, a mile from the trail, to learn the fate of the man, a cripple. His earth-covered dugout by some miracle had withstood the fire. There were no signs of life about. Whether the man had gone out earlier in the week, or had suffered the same fate as our packers, I did not then know. Evening found our little party many miles from camp. We saw the remains of an elk and several deer; also a grouse, hopping about with feet and feathers burned off—a pitiful sight. Men who quenched their thirst from small streams immediately became deathly sick. The clear, pure water running through miles of ashes had become a strong, alkaline solution, polluted by dead fish, killed by the lye. Thereafter we drank only spring water.

Late that night, weary and silent, the men returned to camp and crept into their blankets. Daylight again found us on the trail equipped with packs and food and blankets. About noon we came upon an old white horse, one of our pack string, badly singed, but very much alive, foraging in the creek.

Late one day, the sixth since the great fire, a messenger, besmudged and exhausted, reached us. From him we learned that Wallace and many other towns and villages had burned; that at least a hundred men had lost their lives and that scores were still missing. He had seen many of the dead brought in.

Our crew had been given up as lost. Several parties were still endeavoring to reach us from different points. Ranger Haines with his crew was then several miles back and would cut the trail to take us out. Our packers, he said, had reached safety. The crippled prospector was still among the missing, and we were to search for him. For three days we combed the burned mountains and creeks for the missing man. On the third afternoon, weary and discouraged, we stumbled upon the ghastly remains, burned beyond recognition. His glasses and cane, which we found near, told the mute story of the last, great struggle of the unfortunate man who, had he but known it, would have been safe in his little shack. In a blanket we bore the shapeless thing out to the relief crew.

From Ranger Haines I heard the story of our packers. Shortly after I had left them they had become alarmed. Hastily saddling the fourteen head of horses, they had left the supply camp for Iron Mountain, sixty miles away. Before a mile was covered they realized the fire was coming and that, encumbered with the slow–moving stock, escape would be impossible. They cut the girths and freed the horses, hoping they might follow. Taking a gentle little saddle mare between them, they fled for their lives, one ahead, the other holding the animal by the tail, switching her along. The fire was already roaring behind. On they ran, the panting animal pulling first one, then the other. Hundreds of spark–set fires sprang up beside the trail; these grew into crown fires, becoming the forerunner of the great conflagration. By superhuman effort they reached the summit on the Idaho–Montana state line. Here the fire in sparse timber lost ground. On sped the men down the other side until the fire was left behind. Then miles farther, completely exhausted, they reached a small cabin, where they unsaddled their jaded, faithful little horse, threw themselves into a bunk and fell asleep.

Two hours later the whinnie of the horse awoke them. A glare lighted the cabin. They rushed out; the fire was again all around them! They rescued the little horse from the already burning barn and dashed down the gulch. It was a desperate race for life. Trees falling above shot down the steep slopes and cut off their trail. The now saddleless, frightened little beast, driven by the men, jumped over and crawled beneath these logs like a dog. Two miles of this brought them to some old placer workings and safety. Exhausted they fell. The fire swept on.

They had crossed a mountain range and covered a distance of nearly forty miles in a little over six hours, including their stay at the cabin—almost a superhuman feat.

Returning to Wallace, I learned that the outside world had suffered far more than we. Eighty–nine men had given up their lives in the great holocaust. The hospitals were overflowing with sick and injured. Hundreds had become homeless refugees.

Assigned the task of photographing the scene of the many casualties, I had an opportunity to observe the extent of the appalling disaster and to reconstruct the scene of the last, hopeless stand taken by those heroic, unselfish men who gave their lives that others might live. Still, not all those heroic efforts were hopeless or *vain. Ranger Pulaski, who so valiantly saved all but six of a large crew, has become a national hero, an outstanding figure in the annals of forest history.*

Forest Supervisor Weigle, who for weeks had so tirelessly worked day and night, unselfishly and alone plunged through the very face of the tempest of fire in an attempt to warn the citizens of Wallace of their danger. At last hopelessly trapped, he rushed through a burning mining mill into a tunnel. As the building fell the tunnel caved, threatening to bury him alive. Covering his head with his coat, he crawled out, plunging through the burning wreckage into a tiny creek. In a few hours he had worked his way through the fire to Wallace, there directing and assisting with the dead and injured.

Ranger Danielson, who so courageously led his little crew into an open mining cut on a mountainside, will bear the horrible, purple scars on neck and hands to his grave, as will all those who were with him. Ranger Phillips, Watson, Vandyke, Rock, Bell, and many others saved the lives of hundreds by their cool, timely judgment. Scores of other unsung heroes still live and work among us,
their fortitude a bright and lasting example.

On Big Creek, thirty men lost their lives while others lay prone for hours in the chilling waters of a tiny stream, great forest giants falling around and across them. Here three men were crushed by a falling tree. One of these unfortunates was caught only by the foot. Men a few feet away heard his cries and prayers, but were powerless to assist. He dug and fought to tear away, but the thing which he had come to save held him fast until coma and finally death relieved his sufferings. On Seltzer Creek the ghastly human toll was twenty-nine. An entire crew was annihilated. The men fell as they ran before the merciless fire.

Each scene is a gripping story of almost unparalleled heroism and sacrifice which it would take pages to recount. Our experience as compared with these was tame indeed, insignificant.

More than three decades have passed through the hour-glass of time and nature has long since reclothed the naked landscape with grass, shrubs and trees, but the great sacrifice of human life is not, and can never be, replaced or forgotten.

Forest Supervisors,

Owing to the exceptional climatic conditions which are making the fire danger this season far greater than any ordinary year, I feel that it is essential to greatly strengthen the force of men on all the dangerous districts as long as the present weather conditions continue. It is necessary, in the first place, to retain a strong guard on every fire which is placed under control, until the rains come, to prevent outbreaks resulting from high winds. Several cases have recently occurred where fires once placed under control have broken out due to an insufficient guard. This should be avoided by only gradually reducing the force on each fire as the danger of further outbreak becomes less.

In the second place, it is absolutely necessary to greatly strengthen the patrol. The forests are so dry and fires spread so rapidly that the patrol force of an ordinary season is wholly inadequate to handle the present situation. In the third place, we need to keep on hand where they are immediately available, a strong force of experienced fire fighters who can be brought together quickly and relied upon to do good work.

To meet the conditions on your Forest along the above lines, I want you to use your full discretion in putting on immediately as large a force of temporary laborers, to be retained until the fire danger is over, as is necessary to give you as complete control of the situation on your Forest as possible through this means. I want to emphasize especially the necessity for reducing but slowly the crews employed to bring large fires under control. Keep the best men and when they are no longer needed to guard a particular area, place them at some point where they will strengthen the patrol and be available when the next fire breaks out. The salary and subsistence of all the temporaries employed for these purposes should be charged against "Fire" and will be paid from the special appropriation for extinguishing fires, not from your Forest allotment. This applies equally to men employed for patrol or guarding smoldering areas as to men employed for actual fire fighting.

In case you find it necessary to appoint some of these temporary employees as Forest Guards in order to authorize them to incur expenditures, make arrests and the like, their salaries should for the present be charged against your Forest allotment as has been done hitherto. Please inform me promptly of necessary increases in your Forest allotment to cover such additional appointments and they will be made from the National Forest Contingent as far as possible.

Please use your own judgment fully in carrying out this plan. I will be responsible for finding the necessary funds for putting it into effect. The policy which I want applied on each Forest is to keep as many men on the job as will enable us to fully control the present situation in so far as it can be done by that method.

Very truly yours,

W.B. Greeley
District Forester

Commanding Officer, Fort Harrison
Helena, Montana

Dear Sir:

A wire has been received from the Forester stating that the commanding officers of the posts in Montana have been instructed to cooperate with the Forest Service in the suppression of forest fires. I understand from the commanding officer at Fort Missoula that he has received a similar wire and am writing you in order to secure your suggestions in lining up this work in case it becomes necessary to call upon you for assistance. At the present time the fires are well in hand and are all practically under control and I anticipate that it will not be necessary to request assistance unless continued dry weather and high winds bring about a general conflagration. In order to be able to handle this situation should it occur, I sould like to learn from you how many men you have who could lend assistance and how they will be equipped with pack trains and fire fighting tools, mattocks, shovels, etc.; also how far it would be practical to transport these men away from headquarters.

I should like to have your opinion on whether or not it would be possible in handling the work in the field to have your men under the administrative supervision of a Forest Officer who would direct their work through the commissioned or non-commissioned officers who whould be in immediate charge of the men. I feel that it is essential that a Forest Officer should outline and plan the work and the most practical way in which this could be worked out and yet give your Officers direct charge of the men is the plan outlined above. I would appreciate any suggestions you may have to make an early reply so that we might have this work organized and plans made should it become necessary to ask for assistance.

Very truly yours,

F.A. Silcox
Associate District Forester

After fighting fire all day, these men who saved Lolo Hot Springs marched fourteen miles to begin trenching at a new location. LRD

August 12, 1910

Commanding Officer, Fort Harrison
Helena, Montana

Dear Sir:

In reply to your letter of August 10:
In view of the return to Missoula of a battalion from the American Lake maneuvers, I do not believe it will be necessary to call on you for additional troops from Fort Harrison. If any later developments make this necessary I shall be glad to further communicate with you.

Very truly yours,

F.A. Silcox
Associate District Forester

August 10, 1910

District Forester
Missoula, Montana

Sir:

Reference your letter of the 8th instant, I have the honor to inform you that the maximum number of men that can be sent from this post is 14 privates, two non–commissioned officers and a hospital corpsman. No pack animals at all are on hand, and no wagon transportation can be furnished to go over ten miles or so from the post and in that case only one four–mule wagon.

Sufficient tools in the way of picks, shovels and mattocks for the men who are sent can be supplied. In this connection I would like to be informed what tools are considered most useful.

If men are called for, please let me know the fewest men you can get along with, for what period they should take rations, and as to whether or not tentage other than ordinary shelter tents can be used.

I have telegraphic authority to send men by rail a "reasonable" distance. This term is so indefinite that I would have to ask special authority in case assistance was asked for outside say fifty or seventy–five miles radius of the post.

In regard to handling work and men, I think that your suggestion is the best method to be employed; the commissioned or non–commissioned officer in charge of party confers with the Forest Officer in charge, who lays out the work desired; then the party carries out this work under the immediate charge of its officer. He will make an honest endeavor to give all the assistance desired, but all instructions and requests must past through him.

Very respectfully,

James Hanson
Captain, 14th Infantry

The Helena Independent

BY JNO. S. M. NEILL—ESTABLISHED 1866

Entered at Helena, Mont., as second class matter.

SUBSCRIPTION RATES:

Daily, by carrier, per month.....$ 1.00
Daily, by carrier, per week...... .35
Daily, by mail, including Sunday,
  per year...................... 10.00
Daily, by mail, including Sunday,
  six months.................... 5.00
Daily, by mail, including Sunday,
  three months..... .... 2.50
Sunday edition, by mail, per year 2.50
Semi-weekly edition, by mail, per
  year 2.00

Work for Fighting Men.

From Butte an Associated Press dispatch has gone forth stating that the district forest supervisor will appeal to the war department for the immediate aid of the regular army in fighting the fires which are now devastating great areas of the timbered lands of Montana. The cry for help, belated as it is, is one of the very few reasonable demands that have emanated from the forestry bureau as operated in this state. We believe and contend that these lads in Lincoln green yclept foresters, are an expensive and useless burden to the public. They may be picturesque, but they are not amusing and in their amateur activities they are more of an annoyance than a service. The proper place for the Merry Forester is in comic opera where the stage manager takes care of a papier mache forest, the house fireman puts out an incipient blaze with a hand grenade, and all the merrie crewe have to do is dance, pose, sing and draw their pay.

The Pinchot troupe of foresters now infesting the west should be called in, paid off and abolished. If they are not a nuisance, they are of no practical use in the business of preventing or fighting forest fires. They are untrained, scattered, ignorant of wood-craft in most cases, without discipline and without experience in the real hardships and trials incident to the work of guarding and saving the forests. Careless campers pay little or no attention to the civilian forester. They look upon him as an interloper, a meddler, a joke. They evade him, disobey him, play jokes on him. Probably he is a good-natured college boy got who his job through a pull, or is riding the reserve for his health and the incidental federal voucher. It's a gay life, that of many of these foresters—until the fire stars. Inexperienced, undirected, lacking in equipment and numbers, powerless in the face of the one big task that can confront him, the federal forester now shouts at the war department for soldiers.

Guardianship of the forest reserves comes naturally, logically and economically within the functions of an army of disciplined soldiers. Combat with an onrushing forest fire is fit work for fighting men. Ceaseless vigilance, regular patrols, established stations, perfect discipline, numerical strength, celerity of action, courage, experience and authority are all necessary to the adequate protection of the forests whether in the prevention of incipient fires or in the larger test of downright battle with a raging conflagration.

Manifestly the army, the regular establishment, is the right and available agency for the effective guardianship of the forests. The most widespread and costly forest fire California ever knew was permitted to destroy millions of dollars worth of timber before, as a last resort, the regular army was called upon. The soldiers went at it as they would attack an invading army and subjugated it in a few days. When the Yellowstone National Park first passed from under the control of a civilian superintendent and his amateur assistants, vandalism was rampant in that wonderland of primeval forests, outlandish formations and wild game. The animals were being slaughtered, the forests burned and cut, the beautiful and priceless places and things disfigured and dismantled by the ungoverned visitors.

When Capt. Harris and his company of regular troopers took charge, the vandalism stopped. It has not been resumed. The thoughtless camper has been taught to put out his fires, and if he fails, it is quenched for him. The killing of game, the defacement of the formations, the burning of forests and the dozens of acts of wanton and foolish vandalism that once menaced the famous playground of the people, have all been stopped by military authority. The camper who would jibe at a civilian forester takes off his cap to the uniform of the United States army and obeys orders.

Abolish the forester and put the soldier in charge of the timber wealth of the nation. Let him commence his campaign at the beginning of April and continue on the detail till October or later. The field is big enough and the work important enough to keep an army of occupation usefully busy in the open for at least half the year. The officers on such detail should be paid $10 per month additional; the enlisted men should have $2. The plan would save annually $5,000,000 now wasted by forest fire. It would give healthful, pleasant, educative and useful work to the army. It would enhance the morale of the army, lift it in public estimation, strengthen it in popular esteem, give it a motive as well as an excuse for living in time of peace, do away with the opera bouffe forester and conserve in fact, instead of in theory, the natural timber wealth of the nation.

This editorial in the August 4, 1019, issue of the **Helena Independent** *is a scathing comment on the foresters of the new U.S. Forest Service.*

Ranger Joe Halm's fire crew at the camp on Timber Creek at the headwaters of the St. Joe River in Idaho. Thousands of civilians and soldiers were pressed into service in August, but only a limited number of them had any fire or forest experience. Getting supplies to the fire fighters was a major problem with the primitive means at hand. OHS

Joe Beauchamp's homestead ranch on the Middle Fork of the St. Joe River where ten fire fighters burned to death on August 20. OHS

These interesting fire–related photos were taken by C.H. Shattuck of the Lochsa Ranger District, Clearwater National Forest. LRD

Fire fighters following a fire lane back to their camp at Lolo Hot Springs.

Axe and saw squads going to dinner at Lolo Hot Springs.

Fire fighters at dinner, Lolo Hot Springs, 1910.

Pack string on their way to a fire at Packer Meadows near Lolo Pass.

Axe and sawmen working in advance of the trenchers near Lolo Hot Springs.

Fire camp at Lolo Pass.

Digging a fire line in a fruitless effort to stop the fires.

Loading up a pack string to take supplies to the fire fighters

Haun's Ranger Station in the Lolo National Forest near Haugan, Montana, was in the path of the great fire.

The St. Joe Ranger Station near Falcon, Idaho. Henry Kottkey was the district ranger. This building was destroyed. OHS

St. Joe Ranger Station two weeks after the big fire of 1910. The station was totally destroyed.

This new log home was rebuilt a month after the fire swept through the St. Joe Ranger Station area.

The Aftermath

Weather conditions precipitated the 1910 big burn, and weather conditions ended the fires. On August 22 the winds began to gently fall on most forests in District One, and snow fell on higher elevations. Temperatures dropped. Not all of the fires were extinguished by the cooling moisture, and crews continued to mop up through August. For all intents and purposes, as August ended, so, too, did the big burn.

In the swells of the aftermath, the Forest Service was wiser and, in the long run, better equipped to fight wild fire and manage national forests.

Timber eventually grew back, but much of it was inferior to the original stands. Some forests were replanted. Certain types of soil erosion and insect infestations can be blamed on the 1910 fire.

Railroads became more careful about setting fires along their rights-of-way; the Milwaukee Road was even electrified at a later time. Citizens became more mindful of, and careful with, the use of fire in the national forests. Congress began to appropriate more funds for fire fighting, for fire research, for properly managing the nation's forests.

Parts of the burned areas succored new life forms, as sheep were brought to graze on the fireweed, hollyhock, and other plants that blossomed following the fire.

However, about $13.5 million worth of damage resulted, and about 3,000,000 acres of private and federal forest land burned, totaling 7.5 billion board feet of timber. The lost timber could have been used to construct 50,000-55,000 four-room houses. Another interesting analogy speculates: if one continuous freight train were coupled together with 35,000 board feet per car, that train would stretch 2,400 miles. The cost of fire fighting to the government $800,000.

Even as late as February 1911, a ranger reported finding still-smoking snags sticking up through five feet of snow in the Clearwater country.

In terms of human life, fatalities probably numbered at least 85-7 including 78 employed fire fighters and seven civilians. Seventy-five died in the Coeur d'Alene National Forest—two fire fighters, one prospector, and two people in Wallace. Four were killed in the Cabinet National Forest and two in the Pend Oreille. One civilian died at Taft, Montana, and three homesteaders perished in the Kaniksu National Forest near Newport, Idaho.

The remains of fire fighters who had been temporarily laid to rest where they had fallen were exhumed and placed in cemeteries in Wallace and St. Maries, Idaho.

Wildlife also perished. A former ranger wrote, "If you could see a little bear clinging high in a blazing tree and crying like a frightened child, you could perceive on a very small scale what happened to the forest creatures."

For at least a time people in the nation, and for that matter, even in other countries, realized that hellish fires had burned in Idaho and Montana. Daylight was shut out as far north as Saskatoon, Saskatchewan, Canada; as far south as Denver; and as far east as Watertown, New York. To the west, officers of a British ocean vessel 500 miles out of San Francisco said that they were unable to take observations for ten days because of smoke in the atmosphere caused by the big burn. Some claim that smoke from the big blaze reached one–third of the way around the world.

But the spirit, the will to fight back against disaster, is strong in the West. This intrepidity is reenacted in an article of the *Daily Idaho Press*, August 27, 1910. It stated:

Inside of one year Basil Rizzonelli has been burned out at Falcon, on the Milwaukee Road, three times. The third time occurred when the forest fire [of 1910] swept through that section a few days ago. The loss was about $1250 on the building and lumber, though $1500 worth of supplies was saved.

Mr. Rizzonelli put up a tent following his second fire and has been building the new hotel around it. The structure was partly finished when fire hit that section again and destroyed the building as well as the lumber. The business has been carried on right along despite the calamities that have befallen it.

When asked if he would rebuild the Falcon hotel, Mr. Rizzonelli remarked, "Why, yes, what else can I do? After awhile it will stop burning."

It's inconceivable that a fire of this magnitude will ever again occur in the United States. Smokejumpers, lookouts, aerial detection and retardant planes, much improved communications, better weather forecasting, lightning and fire research and a well developed trail system, would seem to make the chances of such a fire happening again too remote to seriously consider.

Destruction of the forest was complete in many area along the Idaho–Montana border. Notice the log chute on the left. HWP

Destruction along the right–of–way of the Chicago, Milwaukee & Puget Sound (later the Milwaukee Road) in Idaho. PHPC

Description of Fire Killed Timber on St. Regis River
Lolo National Forest

The fire–killed timber on the St. Regis River naturally falls into four logging units, two large and two smaller.

1. All the St. Regis River above Taft. This is estimated at 99,000 M. feet including white pine 20,000 M., mixed species, spruce, larch, red fir, hemlock and lodgepole pine 79,000M. feet. This timber is now being advertised at a minimum stumpage rate of $2.00 per M. It is a very choice body of timber lying in both sides of the N.P. Railroad and before the fire a bid of $4.50 per M. had been received for it. Nearly all killed by fire.

2. Big Creek. Roughly estimated at 120,000 M. feet including about 30,000 M. white pine, balance spruce, red fir, larch and lodgepole pine, both saw and tie timber. About 50% fire–killed, balance only ground burned. Stumpage prices from $2.00 to $3.00 per M. depending on how much green timber is included. Stream drivable for ties but not for saw logs. Would be necessary to build railroad up the creek.

3. Silver Creek. Rough estimate, 10,000 M. feet, Mixed species. One to three miles from railroad. All fire killed.

4. Pacific Creek. Rough estimate 12,000 M. mixed species. Three to four miles from railroad. All fire killed.

Beside these principal bodies there are a number of tie propositions near the railroad. In most cases fire killed tie timber will be sold for 6 cents per tie.

Sluicing in a Milwaukee Railroad trestle on the "Loop" on the North fork of the St. Joe River. Most of this basin and the trestle were burned out. The railroad suffered considerable damage to tracks, bridges and buildings located in the Montana-Idaho divide area. The coal-burning engines caused numerous fires along the railroad right-of-way. Eventually the Milwaukee electrified its line across the mountain in 1914-15, minimizing such hazards.

September 3, 1910

Forest Supervisors:

The American Red Cross has contributed a fund of One Thousand Dollars to be used in paying the expenses for medical attendance and hospital services for men injured or disabled in fighting Forest fires in this District. This fund will be disbursed by me in Missoula and I will be glad to have you send me as rapidly as they are obtainable, any bills which are properly chargeable against it. Expenditures under this fund must be limited to hospital and medical bills, exclusive of expenses for the burial or shipment of bodies.

In submitting any bills which should be paid from this fund please attach a certification over your signature as a Forest Officer as to the correctness of the amounts stated in the bill. It is, of course, essential to protect the Red Cross Society from imposition that the correctness of such accounts be carefully ascertained and checked before they are submitted to me for payment. If such cases are brought to your attention where persons alleging injuries in fire fighting claim to have paid amounts for medical or hospital services which are properly chargeable against this fund, please investigate the cases as fully as possible and submit bills for payment from this fund in all cases which you are satisfied are genuine. Wherever practicable, the original bills from the physician or hospital should be furnished. If this is not possible, an affidavit from the party claiming reimbursement accompanied by your certificate as to the correctness of the charges alleged and the propriety of their being paid from the Red Cross fund will be accepted.

Bills for the care, shipment or disposal of the bodies of the men who lost their lives while fighting fire will be met from the hospital fund at the District Office. This fund will be made up from hospital fees paid by fire fighters and from personal subscriptions from members of the Service. Bills covering expenditures of this character should be submitted as promptly as possible to the District Office.

W.B. Greeley
District Forester

A lookout platform, located on the Bitterroot Divide near the Taft Tunnel along the Montana–Idaho border, is about to topple from the effects of the fire. It is a wonder that the telephone poles remained standing.
OHS

R.H. McKay, left, and Joe Halm, right, on the new trail cut after the fire on the Little North Fork, St. Joe National Forest. McKay was hired by the Forest Service to document the fire's devastation. He had a studio in Missoula, Montana, and was the most prolific photographer of the Western Montana area for almost four decades.

ADDRESS REPLY TO
"DISTRICT FORESTER"

UNITED STATES DEPARTMENT OF AGRICULTURE
FOREST SERVICE
DISTRICT 1

F
CONTROL
Suppression
1910 Fires

HAMMOND BLOCK
MISSOULA, MONTANA

~~District~~ OO - Fire

September 15, 1910

Forest Supervisors:

I think it is worth while to bring to your attention the following extract from the speech of Theodore Roosevelt at Pueblo. I will be glad to have you bring this to the attention of your Rangers.

"I want to call your attention to the wonderful work done by the Forest Service in fighting the great forest fires this year. With the very inadequate appropriation made for the Forest Service, nevertheless that service, because of the absolute honesty and efficiency with which it has been conducted, has borne itself so as to make an American proud of having such a body of public servants; and they have shown the same qualities of heroism in battling with the fire, at the peril and sometimes to the loss of their lives, that the firemen of the great cities show in dealing with burning buildings."

Very truly yours,

W B Greeley

District Forester.

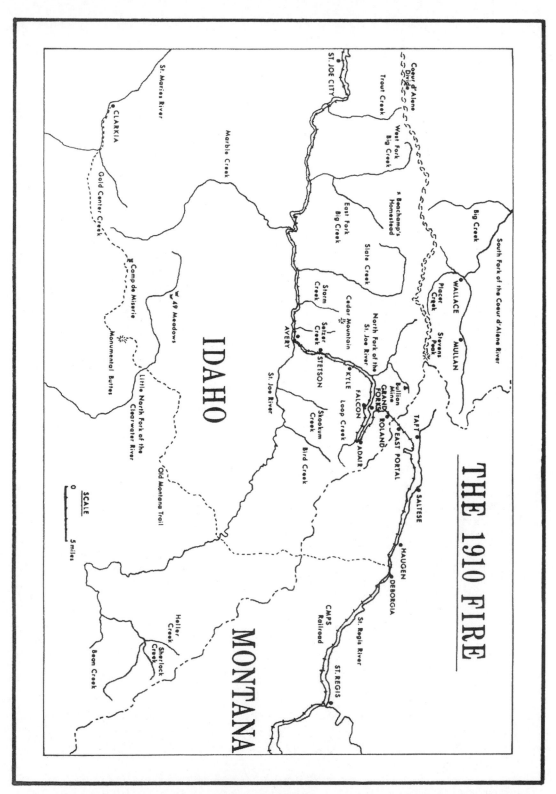

Map from **Up the Swiftwater, A Pictorial History of the Colorful Upper St. Joe River Country,** *reprinted by permission of the Museum of North Idaho, Coeur d'Alene, Idaho.*

The West Fork of Placer Creek in the Coeur d'Alene National Forest after the fire. Not only were trees and wildlife destroyed, but the soil was blackened and fused to a hardened mass. The watershed conditions were greatly affected for many years in the burned areas.

This Halm photo taken in September 1910 shows downed timber near Falcon, Idaho.

This Halm photo shows downed timber and a trail in Shoshone County, Idaho.

Big Cedar Flats on the Little North Fork of the St. Joe River.

Looking east, Big Creek of the St. Joe River.

Giant cedars piled by the force of the wind during the fire on August 20, on the Little North Fork of the St. Joe River.

Ground fire stopped by a trench cut by fire fighters near Graham Creek.

A September 1910 photo showing effects of the fire along the Northern Pacific Railway looking west toward Lookout Pass.

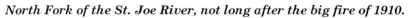

North Fork of the St. Joe River, not long after the big fire of 1910.

185752

The stark reality of a fire's destructive force on Sleepy Ridge in the Wallowa National Forest of Oregon in 1910. The litter and duff have been burned off, and the only remains are blackened poles sticking out of the ground.

AFTER
RES FIRES 1910
OPR 1910
ENGLISH
WALLACE,
IDA.

The way 200,000 acres of the Lolo forest were left by the 1910 fires. This H. English photo was taken in the cedar bottoms of Silver Creek where the trees were blown over by the winds.

Burned timber on Rainy Creek, a tributary of the St. Regis River at the east portal of the Chicago, Milwaukee and & Puget Sound Railroad tunnel.

Burned timber near the Taft Tunnel after the big fire of 1910.

View from the Northern Pacific Railway grade between Borax and Lookout.

Big Cedar Flats on the Little North Fork of the St. Joe River.

Giant white pines in Idaho, killed by the fire.

Original grave on Big Creek of the St. Joe River where seven fire fighters were first buried.

Giant white pine that killed three men during the fire on August 20.

A pit in the side of a creek bed where several men tried to protect themselves from fire the night of August 20.

Bodies of fallen fire fighters disinterred from their original grave on Setzer Creek and prepared for transportation for final burial.

Black soldier's camp, after the fire. These troops of the 25th Infantry from Fort Wright in Spokane County, Washington, fought fires and maintained order in Avery and other towns affected by the fires.
UI 8—CO6

In 1911 and for years after the fire, crews were busy at work seeding the burned–over area. This view shows a crew on the Lolo National Forest sowing ponderosa pine seeds with corn planters.

An eastern white pine, planted in 1910, is shown in this 1922 photo, taken near Sylvanite, Montana, on the Kootenai National Forest,

Burned–over area in the Lolo National Forest.

Logging operations on the Middle Fork of Big Creek in the St. Joe National Forest, shortly after the fires.

The Towns

Men battled the big burn not only in the forests, but also in the towns. The largest and also the most threatened community was Wallace, 13 miles west of the Idaho–Montana border. Wallace's 6,000 residents first became aware of the onrushing forest fire about 2 PM on August 20, when a column of smoke was spotted.

The progress of the fire was relatively slow that afternoon, but it relentlessly bore down on the town from the southwest. Before sunset the wind began to howl. William W. Morris, an assistant in the Coeur d'Alene National Forest in 1910, described that scene from a nearby vantage point:

Never had any of us seen such a wild sight. In the direction of the city of Wallace great masses of smoke were blowing wildly up the great valley of the South Fork. Southward toward the St. Joe River stood a great white cloud pillar, apparently still, looking like a great thunderclap, or the steam cloud that attends the eruption of a volcano. Many of the men thought it was a cloud and predicted rain at last. Westward the sun was setting in a flying black mass, looking like a great red ball of fire. Our high ridge gave us a wonderful view. The weird scene greatly impressed them, and one could not help having the feeling of fear and awe which the scene produced, as if a great tragedy was about to happen. Many fire fighters from other parts spoke of this later. And tragedy was taking place in all these regions.

By 6 PM Mayor Walter Hanson had ordered every able–bodied man to report for fire duty. He threatened them with jail if they disobeyed.

The fire fighters tried to set back-fires and to counter the impending flames, but they were forced to quail before the oncoming killer fire and wind. As the winds increased, fire began in the east end of Wallace at the *Times* newspaper office about 9 that night. Most of the fire had come from Placer Creek Canyon and had swirled over the hills flanking the canyon entrance of town. It hit with an incredible fury. The wind was so strong that the fires jumped over the major section of Wallace and struck at the east end of town, even though they had come from the southwest.

Patients from the Hope Hospital were quickly transferred to the hospital in Osburn, four miles to the west. Providence Hospital, with 25 patients and a like number of sisters, nurses, and attendants, was threatened. They were all crammed into a rescue train of the Northern Pacific Railway which sped them through the burning hills toward Missoula and refuge at St. Patrick Hospital.

People buried possessions in their yards. One family on the edge of town convinced a group of men to help carry their grand piano up the Burke road to an old mine tunnel for safekeeping.

Fires gobbled up telephone and telegraph lines, but before communi-

THE SEATTLE POST-INTELLIGENCER.

VOL. LVIII., NO. 99. SEATTLE, WASHINGTON, MONDAY, AUGUST 22, 1910.—FOURTEEN PAGES—IN TWO PARTS PRICE FIVE CENTS

FOREST FLAMES WREAK HAVOC; $1,000,000 IS LOSS AT WALLACE AND 25 DEAD

Birdseye View of Wallace, Idaho, Before the Fire

IDAHO AND MONTANA TOWNS SUFFER DISASTER

Great Army of Terror Stricken Settlers Are Driven From Their Homes

WALLACE, Idaho, Aug. 21.—Daylight this morning showed the imminent danger of the city's destruction has passed, but it brought also confirmation of losses which were only rumored and suspected during the conflagration of the night. At least two died in the city fire, John Boyd, a pioneer of the Cœur d'Alenes and a former Oregon Railroad & Navigation Company agent, and an unknown man or woman, having incinerated in the Michigan hotel. Only the skull of the latter was found in the ruins this morning.

Toll of Dead Unavailable

Of the fire fighting forces an accurate toll of the dead and wounded is quite unavailable, but the known of the dead number twenty-four, the total injured twenty-five. In addition to two hundred. The steady work of the city fire department, members of the Twenty-fifth infantry, railroad workers and the local forces alone saved Wallace from total destruction. The conflagration in the east end was stayed shortly after 11 o'clock, and back firing in adjoining hills to the west and south prevented the fire in those directions. It is estimated that the loss in the city is over $1,000,000. The entire eastern section from Seventh street to Canyon is destroyed, with three portions of residences on the hillside.

MISSOULA, Mont., Aug. 21.—Merciless and remorseless, the flames in Western Montana and Idaho are sweeping over a vast area, laying hundreds of fugitives before them, destroying small settlements and untold millions of dollars worth of property.

The situation tonight is more serious than it was in the early evening, the story as to Wallace, Idaho, where it is believed that nearly half the city will be saved.

Communication Broken

Communication with Wallace to the west has been possible at intervals today, but eastward it is entirely cut off, and it is known that over one half of the town above Seventh street has been burned. At this a hard fight is being made, and with an improvement in the wind it is hoped that the flames may be driven back in the eastern portion of the city. Missoula is reported at Wallace is a city that has been spared to death.

Lives Lost

Rescuers Organize

Refugees Suffer

Roused From Sleep

Child Born in Car

MANY BELIEVED TO BE CUT OFF BY FLAMES

Twenty Forest Fire Fighters Are Reported to Have Lost Their Lives

SHOOTS WOMAN DOWN IN STREET FULL OF PEOPLE

Thrice Wounded, She Runs and Passersby Seek Safety Behind Poles and Trees

KILLS BROTHER AND NIECE IN SUDDEN FIGHT

Italian Runs Amuck With Knife—Is Shot After Stabbing Many Persons

CAPT. E. B. WOOD IS SLAIN AT SEA BY INSANE PASSENGER

Murderer Then Jumps Overboard From Deck of S. S. Buckman

cation was cut off, Mayor Hanson was able to make a number of important calls. The fire station was ordered to sound the bell for evacuation; from the army the mayor requested troops to help load relief trains; the police chief was advised to open the jail and take prisoners to the city park for safekeeping; and officials from the town of Kellogg were warned that people from Wallace would be coming that way, mostly with only the clothes on their backs.

People scrambled madly to leave the burning town. The exodus toward Osburn and Kellogg to the west was erratic. Some rushed to rescue families, possessions and pets. Others wildly ran to help neighbors and relatives. Still others franticly tried to save records, money, or goods from their businesses. Some possessions had been carefully packed earlier by those who had anticipated the dramatic moment of departure. Some people had bundled up belongings in sheets or old blankets because they had tarried too long and had time to do nothing else. Others were bare-handed, carrying only themselves toward hoped-for safety. Some residents stayed in Wallace, determined not to leave.

Most headed for the railroad yards, where special evacuation trains of the Northern Pacific Railroad and the Oregon, Washington Railroad &Navigation Line had been made up earlier. When the evacuation bell rang, it signalled pandemonium at the railroad yards. People were at their best—and their worst. Men helped women and children into limited space on coach cars. One man roughly pushed a pregnant woman aside and tried to take her place in a coach. The yardmaster threw him off, along with a drunk man. A mother handed her baby to a friend while she clambered aboard. The brakeman slammed the door shut since the car was full; but when he saw what had happened, he opened the door, and the child was quickly handed up to its panicked mother.

Contrary to Mayor Hanson's orders, some able–bodied men jumped on the relief trains. Hanson ordered the 25th Infantry to throw them off. Many of them, however, still clung to the sides of tops of cars and found places in boxcars and flatcars. Some hugged the sides of engines and coal tenders as the trains snaked on their hegira out of harm's way.

While many relief trains headed east toward Kellogg and Spokane, an engine with a caboose came to Kellogg from Saltese, Montana, to the east. This was the train that spirited away the Providence Hospital patients and staff to the east. The train hooked up to a length of boxcars at Mullan and chugged back east across the Bitterroot Range over Lookout Pass, returning to Montana. More people boarded the mercy train at Taft and at Saltese, Montana; the train picked up frightened refugees along the route to Missoula. This and other relief trains dumped 1,000 to 2,000 people per day on the Montana city for several days as homeless refugees were driven from the fiery blazes that threatened to consume them.

Those who stayed behind in Wallace fought all night for their homes and businesses. At midnight Mayor Hanson declared martial law, and troops patrolled the streets to prevent looting. By morning the fires had begun to dissipate, and two thirds of

Wallace, Idaho, just prior to fires of 1910. UI 8–X304

Wallace, Idaho, after the fire, August 20, 1910. PHPC

Wallace, Idaho, after the fire. The brick shell of the Oregon, Washington Railroad & Navigation Company depot stands against the hill, Washington
UI 8-X90

Wallace, Idaho - view from Samuels Hotel after the fire, showing the Oregon, Washington Railroad & Navigation Company depot. August 20, 1910.
UI 8-CO4A

the town had been saved. Probably $1 million worth of property went up in smoke and flames, and two persons were killed—an unidentified man who burned in the Michigan Hotel and Joseph Gastin Boyd of *Wallace* who died trying to rescue his pet parrot from his burning home.

Fortunately, Wallace had a good water supply. Many area newspapers carried this item datelined August 22, Spokane:

Beer is being used at Wallace for drinking purposes in place of water. The water supply ran short Saturday (August 20) for drinking purposes when fire attacked the town and all still and cistern water was turned into the city mains. Mayor Hanson issued orders that none should drink the contaminated water and gave all saloons permission to keep open Sunday.

Other towns were either burned or bypassed, with no apparent pattern. The unpredictable fire storm struck with pitiless fury or not at all. *Mullan*, Idaho, seven miles to the east of Wallace, was unscathed. The town of 1,700 was clearly threatened, with the fire bell ringing constantly and the hose cart of the fire department in continuous use. Home owners used garden hoses to wet down houses and put out fallen brands that came hurtling into town.

Women and children were evacuated by relief train. Members of the citizens' committee patrolled the railroad station area with brickbats and guns. No able–bodied man left Mullan by train. After a while, not everyone was certain that train evacuation was best, anyway. Reports filtered in that the town was surrounded by fire. Perhaps, many reasoned, it would be better to stay in town where chances of survival might be better than taking an eastbound relief train which had to ease across vulnerable trestles and rights–of–way that were but narrow ribbons through heavily forested terrain. A rumor spread that a trainload of people from Wallace had already been trapped and burned to death. Those who had not returned to their homes in response to the rumors and fears soon did so, when word came from the railroad that fire had eaten into the railroad yards at Wallace to the west and no trains could get through. There was no place to go but home. They went, and their town was spared, with the exception of Tent Town where transient miners had lived.

_____

Men burned in the fire, Wallace, Idaho.
UI 8-X545H

Damage to the east end of Wallace, August 20.
UI 8-X545D

Ruins of the Coeur d'Alene Hardware warehouse.
UI 8-X88

Foundry ruins. The cottage on the terrace was the only one left standing in that part of town.

Looking west over the destruction at Wallace, Idaho, after the firestorm of August 20, 1910.

WALLACE RANGER STATION

FLAMES SURROUND IDAHO MINING CAMP

FOREST FIRES ARE WITHIN TWO MILES OF WALLACE AND TOWN IS THREATENED.

Wallace, Idaho, Aug. 11.—(Special)—Wallace is in more danger now from forest fires than she has been at any time this summer. Fires on Placer creek are not more than two miles distant and burning slowly this way while fires on Lake gulch are about a mile and a half distant and are on one slope of the mountain ridge that separates the Wallace valley from Lake gulch. The Slate creek fire travelled four miles today to Placer creek. The flames are going up toward Stevens peak and Mullan tonight. Several small fires were started in the city tonight from burning cinders blown in from the fires. The sidewalks are covered with ashes. The forest supervisor states that if the wind tomorrow is strong the flames will doubtless be blown well toward Wallace.

*The ruins of Wallace, Idaho,
August 20, 1910.*

Ruins of the Sunset Brewing Co. building in Wallace.
UI 8-CO4D

A corner of the Samuels Hotel, on the right, in Wallace. Had it not been for the hotel, courthouse and Worstells being constructed of brick and stone, the entire town would have burned down. UI 8-X92

Avery, Idaho, was a railroad town directly in the path of the big burn. The superintendent and chief carpenter of the Missoula Division of the Milwaukee Road directed the evacuation of the small community. Women and children were sent on their way toward Missoula within 30 minutes. A company of black soldiers of the 25th Infantry stood guard on the platform of the cars as they made their way east. The men of Avery and the balance of the soldiers followed in boxcars.

Part of the community was saved thanks to Thaddeus A. Roe, a ranger, and seven men of Avery who stayed behind after the relief train chugged out of town. They fired the buildings on the outskirts of town and began to force a backfire toward the big blaze. Roe wrote of the wall of fire eating its way down the hillside toward Avery and of the backfire creeping toward the big blowup. When the two met he declared:

Never have I seen anything like it. Plunging at each other like two living animals, the two met with a roar that must have been heard miles away. The tongues of fire seemed to leap up to heaven itself and after an instant's seething sank to nothingness.

We had won, but the strain of those four and a half minutes (the time it had taken for the backfire to meet the main fire) had exhausted us, and we sank down and lay there in the ashes babbling incoherent thanks to God.

The rest of the world didn't know what we were going through. It couldn't, and that was the terrible part of it. We might have been the only men in the world for all it mattered. Alone, we were left nothing but our bare hands and the help of our Creator to bring us out alive.

Avery was the western terminus of a Milwaukee Road section that ran

Avery, Idaho, 1934. LRD

from Deer Lodge, Montana. It was also a center for rescue operations on either side of the Taft tunnel during the 1910 fire

Grand Forks, about midway between Taft and Avery, was a rough–and–tumble town of laborers and camp followers. As the fire storm swept into town, residents raced ahead of it, scurrying for Falcon one mile away. The wild wind–fire quickly lapped up Grand Forks. Next, a telegraph message clicked into nearby Kyle that Falcon, too, was endangered. The work engine sent in relief screamed from Kyle over burning bridge timbers to Falcon and picked up the refugees from Grand Forks and Falcon as fire engulfed that little railroad town.

Engineer Johnnie Mackedon coaxed his train back to Kyle and picked up several people at that settlement, which had also begun to burn. Mackedon then gingerly nudged his mercy train over a fire–weakened trestle between Kyle and Stetson and stopped to rescue the section crew there. Finally the overburdened little train, with men clinging to the locomotive and hanging from the running boards, triumphantly whistled safely into Avery.

Meanwhile, another work train had made a mercy run up the east slope of the Bitterroot Divide to the Taft tunnel, picking up refugees along the way. These nearly 400 homeless people found temporary sanctuary in the two–mile–long tunnel.

Just east of the Idaho–Montana border, the Northern Pacific tracks passed through Borax Siding, Taft, Saltese, Haugan and DeBorgia, and then joined the main line at St. Regis. The towns were in line with the fire storm as it crossed the divide into Montana and spread into the Lolo and Cabinet National Forests.

Grand Forks, Idaho. OHS

Grand Forks, Idaho, one mile from Falcon. Destroyed by the Great Fire of August 21, 1910. OHS

Two weeks after the fire tents had been erected on the townsite.

Taft, DeBorgia, Henderson and Haugan, all along the St. Regis River, were destroyed.

Taft had ballooned to and "end-of–the–track" railroad construction town a couple of years earlier. The town had a population of several thousand during the days of railroad building, which included the construction of the Taft tunnel. But By August 20, 1910, the town had no more than 200-300 people.

As fire coming over Lookout Pass threatened to consume the town on the night of August 20, all women and children were evacuated on the refugee train from Wallace when it wended its way through Taft about midnight.

Ranger J.E. Breen of the Taft Ranger Station, who was determined to save the town, took charge of a group of citizens who proved to be of little assistance. In addition to the fire, firewater was at work in Taft that Saturday night and early Sunday morning. The men were apparently trying to drink the town dry before fire consumed the precious alcohol. The town went up in flames,

except for the hotel, a small building, and some Forest Service lumber. One man—probably drunk—was badly burned and taken to Saltese for medical care. He was left in the care of a friend, who also had too much to drink, and as a result, the friend accidently ignited the burned man's bandages with a match. The unfortunate man was set afire for a second time, and he subsequently died. His was the only death in the Lolo forest.

At the time the Wallace–Missoula relief train came through DeBorgia, fire danger was not imminent; consequently no passengers boarded. But before dawn Sunday morning (August 21), town constable and hotel and bar owner Joseph A. Mayo was warned that the fire was closing in, making evacuation necessary. Mayo ordered a relief train which steamed in from Missoula. Lolo Supervisor Elers Koch swung down from the train and tried to organize a crew to set backfires. But it was too late for that, as Koch soon realized, and everyone was ordered to board the harried relief train when it returned from its mission to neighboring

Haugan. The order was obeyed except by a few people who stayed and successfully kept their property from burning to the ground. Joe Mayo's memoirs, however, claim that the few buildings were saved not necessarily by people, but by "freak-est winds." Three or four building survived, while the rest of the town's sixty–eight building were consumed.

Most Haugan residents eagerly clambered aboard the Missoula–bound iron horse panting at the siding, ready to speed them to hoped–for safety. A few laggards stayed in the hotel bar, vowing to deplete the liquor supply before the fire depleted them. At the last minute they boarded the train, apparently with the hotel owner waving a liquor bottle at the fleeting flames which seemed to follow them all the way to St. Regis, several miles to the east. The town was leveled.

Saltese, to the east, wasn't threatened until the afternoon of August 21 (Sunday). Several fire fighting crews were trying to save the town when a work train from Missoula lumbered in. It was en route to Wallace, but could not get there because of burned–out bridges. The section crew refused to work, and they were joined by a group of "toughs" who had been picked up as refugees. The two groups commandeered the work train down the tracks toward Missoula. Soon they returned, blocked by burned bridges to the east. Since bridges had been eaten away both east and west of town, they were forced to join in fighting for Saltese's life to save their own necks. Backfires were set and buildings were hosed down, forcing the fire to skirt the town.

The fire that consumed one–third of Wallace and destroyed Taft, Haugan, Henderson and DeBorgia swept north in the Cabinet National Forest, crossed the Clark Fork Valley, jumped the river, and finally ran itself out in the Kootenai Forest of northern Montana.

Before the hurricane–fire spent itself in the Kootenai National Forest, it threatened but never reached the town of Libby, for the sated maniac was dead.

Harry English photo of Taft, Montana, in 1908. PHPC

View of DeBorgia, Montana, on the line of the Northern Pacific Railway, approximately 88 miles west of Missoula. It was totally destroyed. PHPC

DeBorgia after the fire. The saloon was one of the few buildings left intact. The flames destroyed the railroad towns of Taft and Haugen and threatened Saltese, St. Regis and Superior. PHPC

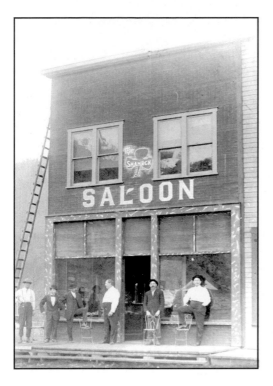

Pre-fire scenes in DeBorgia.

The Savanac Nursery near Haugen was, at one time, the largest forest nursery in the United States. It was right in the path of the fire.

The buildings were all burned, but rebuilding started immediately.

Legacy of the Fires

Graves of 34 fire fighters lost in the great fire can be found in the St. Maries Cemetery, St. Maries, Idaho.

"Unknown
Died August 20, 1910
Big Creek, Idaho" DS

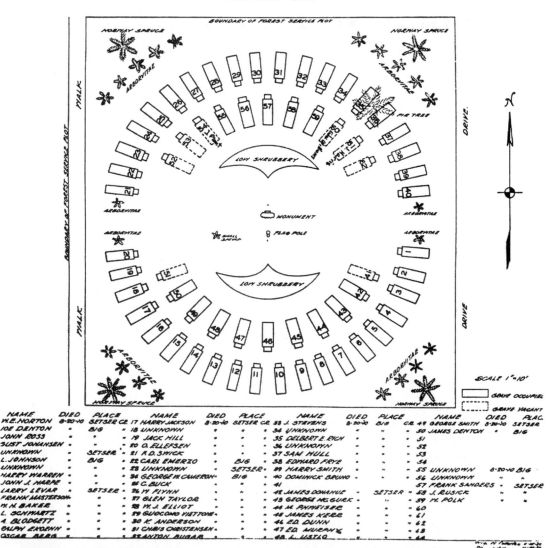

WOODLAWN CEMETERY
ST. MARIES IDAHO

NAME	DIED	PLACE	NAME	DIED	PLACE	NAME	DIED	PLACE	NAME	DIED	PLACE
W.E. NORTON	8-20-10	SETSER CR.	17 HARRY JACKSON	8-20-10	SETSER CR.	33 J. STEVENS	8-20-10	BIG	49 GEORGE SMITH	8-20-10	SETSER
10E DENTON	"	BIG	18 UNKNOWN	"	"	34 UNKNOWN	"	"	50 JAMES DENTON	"	BIG
JOHN ROSS	"	"	19 JACK HILL	"	"	35 DELBERT E. RICH	"	"	51		
SUST JOHANSEN	"	"	20 O. ELLEFSEN	"	"	36 UNKNOWN	"	"	52		
UNKNOWN	"	SETSER	21 R.D. SWICK	"	"	37 SAM HULL	"	"	53		
L. JOHNSON	"	BIG	22 CARL EMERZO	"	BIG	38 EDWARD FRYE	"	"	54		
UNKNOWN	"	"	23 UNKNOWN	"	SETSER	39 HARRY SMITH	"	"	55 UNKNOWN	8-20-10	BIG
HARRY WARREN	"	"	24 GEORGE W. CAMERON	"	BIG	40 DOMINICK BRUNO	"	"	56 UNKNOWN	"	"
JOHN J. HARPE	"	"	25 C. BUCK	"	"	41			57 FRANK SANDERS	"	SETSER
LARRY LEVAR	"	SETSER	26 M. FLYNN	"	"	42 JAMES DONAHUE	"	SETSER	58 J. RUSICK		
FRANK MASTERSON	"	"	27 GLEN TAYLOR	"	"	43 GEORGE McGURK	"	"	59 M. POLK		
M.H. BAKER	"	"	28 W.J. ELLIOT	"	"	44 M. PAYMEISER	"	"	60		
L. SCHWARTZ	"	"	29 GUOCOMO VIETTONE	"	"	45 JAMES KERR	"	"	61		
A. BLODGETT	"	"	30 K. ANDERSON	"	"	46 ED. DUNN	"	"	62		
CALPH EXORNN	"	"	31 CHRIS CHRISTENSEN	"	"	47 ED. MURPHY	"	"	63		
OSCAR BERG	"	"	32 ANTON BUGAR	"	"	48 L. USTLO	"	"	64		

SCALE 1" = 10'

GRAVE OCCUPIED

GRAVE VACANT

Grave monuments in the Nine Mile Cemetery near Wallace, Idaho, erected by the U.S. Forest Service in 1921 for fire fighters who died on Bullion Creek. The top circle is located in the Grand Mound area, the bottom in the Catholic area. DS

THE GREAT FIRE OF 1910

IN AUGUST 1910, THIS AREA WAS RAVAGED BY ONE OF A
SERIES OF HUGE FOREST FIRES WHICH SWEPT THE INLAND
EMPIRE AT THAT TIME. SMALL FIRES HAD BEEN BURNING
FOR DAYS IN TIMBER PARCHED BY A RECORD DROUGHT.
DESPITE THE EFFORTS OF HUNDREDS OF FIRE FIGHTERS TO
CONTROL THE FIRES, GALE FORCE WINDS FANNED SMALL
FIRES INTO BIG ONES. AN ESTIMATED THREE MILLION
ACRES WERE DEVASTATED BY THE 1910 FIRES.

WHILE FIGHTING THE HUGE FIRES, FOREST RANGER
EDWARD C. PULASKI AND HIS CREW OF 45 MEN WERE
TRAPPED BY THE FLAMES. HE LED HIS CREW INTO AN
ABANDONED MINE TUNNEL AND HELD THEM THERE UNTIL
THE FIRE PASSED. SIX MEN DIED, BUT PULASKI'S PROMPT
ACTION SAVED THE OTHER MEMBERS OF THE CREW.

THE TUNNEL IN WHICH PULASKI AND HIS MEN TOOK
REFUGE IS ABOUT 2 MILES UPSTREAM ON THE WEST FORK
OF PLACER CREEK.

USDA - FOREST SERVICE
IDAHO PANHANDLE NATIONAL FORESTS

In 1984 a monument and sign were dedicated to the memory of the dead fire fighters by the U.S. Forest Service near Wallace, Idaho. They are located one–half mile south of Wallace at the mouth of the West Fork of Placer Creek.

PHPC

This stone with tablet is on the grounds of the Savanac Nursery Historic Site at Haugan, Montana, on the Lolo National Forest.

Idaho historical sign just off of Interstate 90 near the Idaho–Montana border at Lookout Pass.

Men Who Lost Their Lives in the 1910 Fires

On Setzer Creek

1. George Smith
2. George Blodgett
3. James Kerr
4. Harvey Jackson
5. L. Rustic
6. James Donahue
7. Frank Sanders
8. Larry Levar
9. M. Phweiser
10. J. Rusick
11. M. Dilo
12. Jack Hill
13. Oscar Berg
14. Ed Murphy
15. Harly Siphers
16. Ralph Ekhoen
17. Frank Getchell or Sketchell
18. Ed Dunn
19. Frank Polic
20. L. Schwartz
21. H.W. Baker
22. Frank Masterson
23. George McGurk
24. O. Ellefson
25. F.D. Swick
26. W. Polk
27. William Casey

At the Dittman Cabin - On the West Fork of Big Creek

1. Gust Johnson
2. W. Flynn
3. Sam Hull
4. L. Johnson
5. Edward Frye
6. John Hoss
7. Harry Smith
8. Joseph Denton
9. J. Stevens
10. John J. Harpe
11. Chris Christensen
12. James Denton
13. Glen Taylor
14. K. Anderson

15.-19. All unidentified. It is believed that one of them was Harry Warren. Three other bodies were found during the summer of 1911, probably homesteaders. One of these was positively identified as Delbert E. Rich.

On the Middle Fork of Big Creek - At the Beauchamp Cabin

1. George W. Cameron
2. Giacomo Viettone
3. Domenico Bruno
4. W.J. Elliott
5. Anton Bucar
6. Carl Omerzu
6. C. Buck

In addition, homesteaders Roderick A. Ames, Joseph Beauchamp and Upton B. Smith lost their lives at or near the same place.

At the Bullion Mine

1. Aaron Benson
2. S.D. Adams
3. Louis Holmes
4. Thomas Welch
5. Ernest Elgin
6. C. Val Nicholson
7. Leslie Zellers
8. Larry Ryson

Appendix

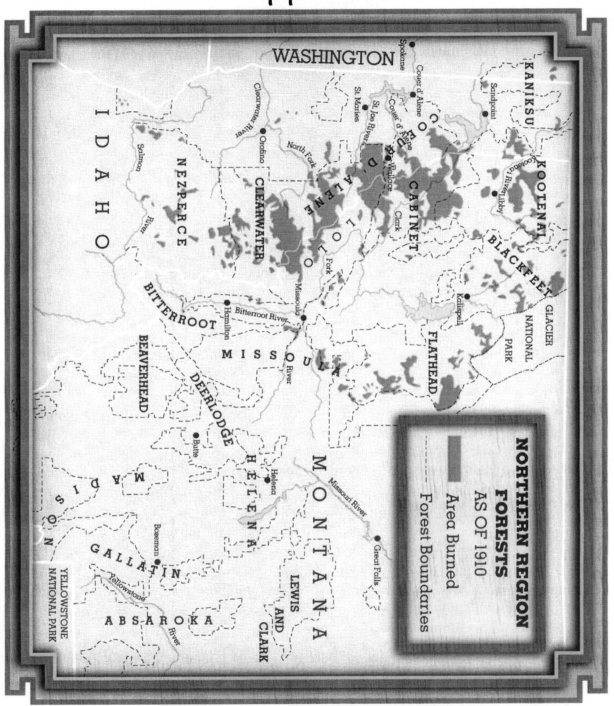

Map by Ken Barnedt and courtesy the **Missoulian.**

The 1910 Fire Season
by Elers Koch

No one can claim to be a real old–timer in the Forest Service unless he went through the 1910 fire season. We have had bad fires since, but nothing approached the terrific burning conditions of the two days of August 21 and 22, 1910. After a long drought period beginning in March, conditions became more and more critical. Springs dried up, and the fuels in the forest were ready to ignite almost spontaneously. Dry lightning storms scattered numerous fires through the undeveloped wilderness country of North Idaho and western Montana. The inadequate forces of the Forest Service battled the flames stubbornly through July, getting some of the fires and being driven back on others.

Finally the climax came. With the humidity down to almost nothing, the southwest fire wind from the Snake River desert whipped into a gale that lasted two days. Hundreds of fires that had been burning for days picked up and joined in the advance of the terrific sweep of fire which roared out of the wilderness forests of the Clearwater, St. Joe and Coeur d A'lene country in Idaho, across the Bitterroot Mountains into Montana to a distance of 40 or 50 miles. The sky turned first a ghastly, ominous yellow, then darkness shut down in the middle of the afternoon. When all was over a large part of the town of Wallace had burned. Saltese, Haugan, DeBorgia and numerous ranches and ranger stations were left in ashes. Eighty–seven men lost their lives in the flames. Game animals were killed by the thousands and the stream bottoms were white with the bellies of dead trout. Billions of feet of fine timber had burned, and millions of acres left a blackened waste. Missoula was filled with refugees from the Coeur d'Alene branch who escaped on the last train out.

I was supervisor of the Lolo Forest at the time. In the night of August 21 the telephone bell at my bedside awakened me. It was Ranger Kottke at Wallace. "Mr. Koch," he said, "the fires have all gone wild. The flames are just breaking into Wallace. I don't know where my family is and my men and pack strings are all out in the path of the fire, and I am afraid many of them can't escape alive." A little later Ranger Haun called from Saltese. He said the hills were all afire around town and he had 200 fire fighters there trying to save the town. Just then communications ceased. The Coeur d'Alene lines were down. In the morning I went out with a special Northern Pacific train down the Coeur d'Alene branch to see what could be done. About three in the afternoon we pulled into DeBorgia. The head of the big fire had just reached the town, and some of the buildings were afire. It was black dark and everybody was carrying lanterns. We loaded the residents of the town on the train and started back down. Between Henderson and St. Regis the whole canyon was afire on both sides and the train had to run through it. The heat was so great that we couldn't stand in the open door of a box car, but fortunately we made it through to St. Regis. About midnight weather conditions changed. The wind continued to blow, but the humidity picked up, and the fires made little progress the next day. The night of August 22 came a general rain.

It is possible that such burning conditions might again occur, but with the present organization of the Forest Service it is not likely that sufficient fires will ever again be uncontrolled at one time to build up such a wide spread conflagration.

October 14, 1910

Forest Supervisors,

　　The financial situation of the District and, through it, of the entire Forest Service is extremely serious owing to the deficit which has incurred for fire fighting expenses. The payments of fire bills previously made together with the vouchers now awaiting payment in the District office will exceed the allotment for fire fighting purposes by $550,000. It is essential therefore that the most careful attention be given to all fire expenditures and to all matters connected with the winding up of the fire accounts in order to avoid any more serious embarrassment of the Service than is absolutely necessary.

　　Special pains must be taken not to charge against "fire" expenditures which are properly chargeable against "general expenses" or "improvements." Very careful investigation of all doubtful charges must be made before they are submitted for payment. In no cases should amounts properly chargeable to lumber companies or private cooperators of any character be paid by the Forest Service, with the expectation of subsequent reimbursement by the cooperator. In such transactions, the amounts paid by the Service increase our fire deficit, and although the account may be ultimately squared with the government as a whole, it is recorded against us as an expense in excess of our allotment. Our present situation is so critical that we must simply require the payees in such cases to wait, until their bills can be paid by the cooperating parties to whom they are properly chargeable.

　　Any fire bills of a doubtful character should be referred to the District office with a full explanation before they are certified for payment. While we must of course meet all obligations incurred during the fire season, the present status of Service finances makes it imperative that questionable bills be disallowed.

　　In order that I may keep closely informed as to the outstanding bills to be paid for fire expenses, please send me a further report by night telegram, immediately upon the receipt of this letter, stating as closely as you are able to ascertain the unpaid fire bills on your Forest which have not yet been submitted to the District Fiscal Agent. Please also report immediately by night telegram any subsequent changes in the estimate, involving an amount of $500 or more, one way or the other. I need constantly specific information, corrected to date, on the outstanding liabilities for fire expenses, and will ask your hearty cooperation in furnishing me with such information.

Very truly yours,

W.B. Greeley
District Forester

GLORE: LADIES AND GENTLEMEN - Today, August 20th, is the anniversary of a date as tragic as any in the history of Montana. Thirty–nine years ago today was the beginning of the St. Joe Forest fire, the worst fire in the history of the United States Forest Service. Conditions in the forests at present are almost as dangerous as those which led up to the St. Joe fire. That fire burned a strip of forest in Montana and Idaho roughly the size of a strip as wide as from Missoula to Stevensville and as long as from Missoula to Helena. The dead timber is still evident on either side of U.S. Highway #10 by the time one gets a little west of St. Regis. We on the Highlander Stagparty, with the active blessing of the sponsors, and all knowing a man can have no finer hobby than a love of the forests and the fish and game they preserve, have brought for guests today Mr. E.H. Myerick, Supervisor of the Lolo National Forest, and Mr. Joe Halm, who went through the St. Joe fire and still wonders how he did it. Mr. Halm, what is a forest fire like?

Halm: One can hardly describe it. It has the noise of a cyclone and the heat of a volcano. It seems to be everywhere at once.

Glore: How did you happen to be in the fire?

Halm: There were numerous small fires that preceded the big fire, and there were many crews on them. I was out with a crew. The wind came up on the 20th of August and took all fires out of control. That is why this is considered the starting date of the fire.

Glore: The wind got the fire out of control by making it crown?

Halm: That's right.

Glore: Exactly what do you mean by crowning?

Halm: That is when the fire leaves the ground and burns through the tops of the trees. Once a fire starts to crown there is not much we can do about it if conditions are bad.

Glore: A crown fire, then, is the most dangerous of all?

Halm: Yes.

Glore: How many men did you have in your crew?

Halm: Sixty–five.

Glore: Did they all get out safely?

Halm: Yes, they followed instructions, and we all got out alive. The people who were burned were those who wouldn't do what the men in charge told them to do.

Glore: The timber that was lost was mostly white pine?

Halm: Yes. A stand over 100 years old. I think the Milwaukee Railroad had ex-pected to take out the timber. That was one reason for building the road, so people said. The timber had never been logged.

Glore: What was the greatest handicap you had in trying fight the fires?

Halm: There were no trails or roads, and we had to go in 65 miles to get to the fire when we were first sent out. In those days one spent the first week trying to get to the fire. It took more time to get into the country than to put out a small blaze.

Glore: How did you and the men keep from being burned alive after you were trapped?

Halm. We got into a little creek and stayed in the water. The timber fell all around us, but by good fortune, no one was struck. It was a wonder that any of the crew got out alive.

Glore: I understand that it was about two weeks before your people knew you were all right?

Halm: Yes, that is right.

Glore: Didn't you tell me that your obituary was published in one of the papers?

Halm: Yes, I brought it along. Doesn't very often happen a man comes home to attend his own funeral.

Glore: What do you recommend be done to people who carelessly leave campfires or flip cigarettes in the woods?

Halm: I'd sentence them to fighting on a few fire fighting crews. I don't think they'd ever do it again.

Glore: Mr. Myerick, what was the timber destruction in the St. Joe fire?

Myerick: Value set at the time was 15 million dollars. I would triple that for present values—say about 50 million dollars. The area burned was about 3,000 square miles, and six billion board feet at least were destroyed. One entire crew of 30 men who disregarded safety orders were completely burned.

Glore: Thirty years ago, of course, you had no such organization and equipment as now.

Myerick: No. We had no trucks and no planes and hardly any roads or trails. During a period of 10 days we had 1,400 CCC boys on several small fires and on the Lochsa fire, and because they were trained for the work, not one of them was injured.

Glore: I suppose you consider the cost of the Forest Service Fire control cheap insurance for what the Service protects.

Myerick: I certainly do.

Glore: Thank you, Mr. Myerick, and thank you Mr. Halm.

A Tool for the Times*

He probably should be forgotten by now. But Ed Pulaski put his name in the annals of history with an invention, the pulaski—although getting credit for it was nearly as futile as the attempt for the Carnegie Hero Award.

Just how and when the pulaski tool was born hasn't been determined. One account says that the Collins Tool Company exhibited something very well like it—an ax and mattock combined on one handle—at the 1876 Centennial. Another account credits a Ranger McPherson with hand–tooling one back in 1906. Another says that in February of 1910, half a year before the Coeur d'Alene fire, Joe Halm and Ed Holcomb, acting under instructions from Forest Supervisor W.G. Weigle, made the tool in Pulaski's blacksmith shop in Wallace. Regardless of who first made the tool, it was Pulaski who saw its possibilities. It was Pulaski who took it to the supervisors' meeting in 1911 where it was "viewed without enthusiasm." It was Pulaski who, undaunted, tinkered with it and gave it birth or rebirth, whatever the case may be.

By 1913 he's made an ax/mattock tool with fairly good balance. A year later he decided to patent it, hoping to make enough money to defray his medical costs. By that time he saw small chance of getting any from the Carnegie Commission.

Mayer Wolff wrote the U.S. Patent Office on Pulaski's behalf to ask about patenting procedures. Several days later a response came—seven pages of patent specifications in minute detail. Wolff sent the memorandum to Pulaski, who wrote back, "I do not see any use of proceeding, as I do not intend spending the money necessary to procure the patent. The tool, it is true, has not been demonstrated to show it has any value, and the only way to prove its worth is take it out and try it as I have done. I think we will let the matter drop for the present at least."

By 1920 the tool was being used throughout the region. But not until after Pulaski's death in 1931 was there further mention of patenting it. That year C.K. McHarg, regional forest inspector, wrote to the Patent Office, "In view of the fact that the Pulaski tool has been standardized and is apt to be manufactured and purchased in large quantities, it would seem that the article should be patented . . . . It is barely possible that some outside interests will endeavor to patent this tool unless some action is taken. I can personally vouch for the fact that Pulaski had the idea and worked up several models as early as 1913 . . . . Any benefits . . . in the form of royalties . . . would assist Mrs. Pulaski very materially.

McHarg's hopes of getting royalties for Mrs. Pulaski were never realized. According to patent law, if an invention had been in use for more than two years prior to application for a patent, the inventor lost his right to patent it. Pulaski had not acted in time.

But there was a way around this. The long memorandum McHarg received from the Patent Office suggested a statute under which the pulaski might be patented. It pertained specifically to patents awarded to government officers for inventions used in the public service. Although Pulaski had forfeited royalties by not acting in time, this statute at least made it possible to put his name on the tool he invented.

The fact that he never received any royalties probably mattered little to Pulaski once his medical bills were paid. As McHarg once wrote, "There was to him nothing in being acquisitive, for mere acquisition gratified nothing in his make up . . . . He had pride in the skill of his hands. Satisfaction came to him from applying that skill to something rough and making it into something useful."

It probably wouldn't even matter to this clearly uncommon man that his name now stands for a common tool. It was the tool, not its name that was important to him. He took something rough and shaped it into a pulaski.

And it looks as if the pulaski is here to stay.—Terry Brenner.

*Printed with permission of the Wallace District Mining Museum.

This large mural depicting Edward Pulaski saving his fire fighters was painted by James R. Buckham and donated to the Wallace Mining Museum by Harry Magnuson. James R. Buckham was born and raised in Wallace, Idaho. He received his Bachelor of Arts in Fine Arts from Gonzaga University in Spokane, Washington, working under the tutelage of Robert Gilmore. He lives and works in the Inland Northwest and is represented in several regional and national collections, both private and institutional. He has worked in several medias, most recently several larger public sculptural projects of granite and basalt.

Postscript

by Dr. William R. Moore
Retired Chief of Fire Management
U.S. Forest Service, Northern Region

That fires burned some three million acres of Montana and Idaho forests in 1910 was nothing new in the evolution of natural systems. Fire had, since vegetation followed the last ice 10,000 years before, cleansed forests and assured perpetuation of plants and animals. If flames and smoke and death and birth by fire were common phenomena, what then was unusual about the "Big Burn" described and illustrated in this book?

In the settling of the west, man's habitation had for the first time collided with forest fire on the rampage, one of the most powerful natural forces at work in the northern Rocky Mountains.

During 1910 the pioneers learned they couldn't manage resources or even inhabit the mountains safely without first dealing with fire. That a repeat of the 1910 holocaust could not be tolerated was obvious, so in the "Big Burn's" smoky aftermath the U.S. Forest Service and companion federal, state and local agencies launched programs to banish fire from the forests. Since then many men and a few women have dedicated—and some have given— their lives to achieve that mission.

No other band of conservationists in America have created history more laden with heroism and adventure. And they won their war against fire; 750,000 acres burned around the turn of the of the century, approximately 25,000 acres are burned today during an average year within the boundaries of the Forest Service's northern region.

But today's perceptive forest manager knows that in conquering an enemy, we have destroyed a friend whose presence in the ecosystem is as essential as the wind and rain. In the absence of fire, forests in the northern Rockies create debris far faster than it can be decayed by climate. Several important shrubs and trees depend on fire for their regeneration. Fire's random flames design diverse mosaics both pleasing and helpful to wildlife. Soil nutrient availability and a host of lesser factors depend on fire in one way or another. And there is growing evidence that even smoke from forest fires is beneficial in controlling certain diseases that attack trees.

So fire can be good or bad depending on the objectives sought in managing our mountain lands. Fire need no longer be viewed as an enemy to be banished at all times in all places. Instead it should be managed to compliment the objectives sought on the land; sometimes vigorously controlled, at other times nurtured to allow enrichment of the ecosystems.

This more professional view of fire forms a welcome landmark in conservation history. But I am grateful that the authors have reminded us that fire on the loose can destroy the objectives of man; indeed can destroy man himself. In this story of 1910 lies warning that all programs designed to allow the fire a freer role must also include preparations to assure that the fire can be controlled should it threaten to spread beyond the intent of the management plan.

Condon, Montana
January 1978

Bibliography

-----*100 Years of Federal Forestry.* Information Bulletin No. 402, Washington, D.C.

Cowen, Charles. *The Enemy Is Fire.* Superior, Seattle, 1961.

Crowell, Sandra S and David O. Asleson. *Up the Swiftwater, A Pictorial History of the Colorful Upper St. Joe River Country.* Museum of North Idaho, publishers.
Braun– Brumfield, Ann Arbor, 1980.

-----*Early Days in the Forest Service, Volumes 1- 4.* U.S. Department of Agriculture, Forest Service, Northern Region, Missoula. N.d.

El Hult, Ruby. *Northwest Disaster.* Binfords & Mort, Portland, 1960.

-----Historic files, 1910 fire. U.S. Department of Agriculture, Forest Service, Northern Region, Missoula. N.d.

Holbrook, Stewart H. *Burning an Empire: The Story of American Forest Fires.* Macmillan, New York, 1944.

Kirkwood, J.E. "Observations in National Forests & Elsewhere During the Summer of 1910." Manuscript, U of Montana, Missoula.

Little, John J. "The 1910 Forest Fires in Montana and Idaho: Their Impact on Federal and State Legislation." M.A. thesis, U of Montana, Missoula, 1968.

MacLean, Norman. *Young Men and Fire, A True Story of the Mann Gulch Fire.* U of Chicago, 1992.

Mayo, Joseph A. Unpublished memoirs. N.d.

-----Newspapers: *Chronicle* (Spokane), *Daily Idaho Press* (Wallace), *Evening News* (Butte), *Missoulian* (Missoula), *News* (Mullan), *News* (Wardner), *Post–Intelligencer* (Seattle), *Spokesman–Review* Spokane), *Standard* (Anaconda), *Star* (Washington, D.C.) *Times* (Seattle).

Space, Ralph S. "The Clearwater Story." U.S. Department of Agriculture, Forest Service, Northern Region, Missoula, 1964.

Spencer, Betty Goodwin. *The Big Blowup.* Caxton, Caldwell, Idaho, 1956.

-----"When the Mountains Roared." U.S. Department of Agriculture, Forest Service, Northern Region, Missoula. N.d.

Index

About Authors

Don Miller was a native of South Dakota and held bachelor and masters degrees from the University of South Dakota. He was a professor of journalism at the University of Montana for many years and up until his death in January 1993 was a professor of journalism at Montana Tech. He was one of the founders of the Historical Museum at Fort Missoula and a former president of the Western Montana Ghost Towm Preservation Society. Mr. Miller authored numerous magazine articles and many historical books on ghost towns of the west.

Stan Cohen is a native of West Virginia and a graduate of West Virginia Univeristy. He spent seven summers working for the U.S. Forest Service in Oregon, Montana, Idaho and Alaska. He founded Pictorial Histories Publishing Co., Inc. in 1976 and has authored or co-authored 69 books and has published 275 to date. He resides in Missoula with his wife Anne.

It took a summer snowstorm to put out the fires on August 24. FRANK HOUDE COLLECTION

Trail Project Description

The Pulaski Tunnel Trail offers both the beauty and peace of a cool walk in a forested canyon by a cascading creek and an adventure into the past. The trail begins at a well-marked trailhead about a half-mile south of Wallace, soon after King Street leaves Wallace's city limits. The trail's two-mile course ultimately brings hikers to a spot across the creek from the historic Pulaski Tunnel, the abandoned mine where "Big Ed" Pulaski saved all but six of his 45-man firefighting crew in the Great Fire of 1910. The site's peaceful and idyllic setting belies the terrible events that etched this place into history almost a hundred years ago.

Until 2003, the trail was lost in overgrowth and erosion. The only signs of its former existence were two historical markers placed across the road from what is now the trailhead. A concerned citizens group organized to save the trail in October of 2002. Since 2003 the trail has been given new life. It has been cleared, graded, and where necessary, strengthened by durable engineering. It has also been equipped with twelve large-format porcelain interpretive signs and a number of bridges where the trail crosses the creek. During the spring and summer of 2010, a trailhead sign will be erected and development of the destination will take place. At the overlook to the mine portal, a rock wall and a pole fence will be installed. The mine portal will be recreated to represent the look of the mine just after the 1910 fire based on historical photographs. Other trail improvements are also planned.

Both the trail and the mine are listed on the National Register of Historic Places.

Courtesy of the Pulaski Project, a division of the Greater Wallace Community Development Corporation. ron@roizen.org

THE PULASKI TUNNEL TRAIL

Mt. Pulaski
5,348 feet
(1,630 m.)

War Eagle Mine

Pulaski Tunnel

Wallace

~ MAP KEY ~

TRAILHEAD
PARKING
TOILET
INTERPRETIVE SIGNS
BRIDGE
BOARDWALK
MINE SITE
OVERLOOK

1/4 mile (1,320 feet)
402.4 meters

~ TRAIL ELEVATION PROFILE ~

(Distance in miles)
(Feet above sea level)

Pulaski Tunnel Overlook Loop
3,720'
Trailhead to 3,800': gradual climb (rise in feet) is 500 feet
Bridge 3 3,600'
Bridge 4 3,500'
War Eagle Mine 3,400'
Bridge 2 3,200'
Boardwalks 3,100'
Bridge 1 3,000'
Pulaski Tunnel Trailhead 0 ml.

1.75 ml.   1.5 ml.   1.35 ml.   1 ml.   0.75 ml.   0.6 ml.   0.35 ml.   0 ml.

Welcome to the Pulaski Tunnel Trail

The beautiful trail offers a scenic, rewarding hiking experience and recounts the dramatic events of the "Great Fire of 1910."

The trail's two-mile course ends at an overlook across the creek from the historic Pulaski Tunnel, the abandoned mine where "Big Ed" Pulaski saved all but six of his 45-man firefighting crew in the "Big Burn." Along the trail are burnt-out cedar stumps, snags, and logs still bearing scars from that catastrophic fire.

- Both the trail and the mine are listed on the National Register of Historic Places. The Pulaski Trail honors the courage, dedication, and self-sacrifice of brave firefighters past, present, and future.

- The trail's first 250 yards (228.6 m.) are paved, wheelchair accessible, and relatively level.

- The rest of the trail is rocky in places and has an increase of 500 feet (244 m.) in elevation from trailhead to end.

- The trail's rated difficulty is MODERATE with the steeper sections near the end.

- A round-trip hike takes between two and three hours.

- Temperatures can vary greatly along the trail – please dress accordingly.

- Sturdy footgear is advised.

- Bring adequate liquids and snacks.

- Twelve interpretive signs are positioned along the trail.

- Other landmarks along the trail include five bridges, three boardwalks, benches, four gabion dams, and the War Eagle Mine.

- The Pulaski Tunnel Trail is open year-round.

Evacuation from 1910 fire recalled by son of early-day family

by Frank Bell

Far Western Montana, on the route to Idaho via Lookout Pass, has bounced back from disaster. The great fire of 1910, a holocaust which leveled three million acres of prime forest, set back development of the area for many years.

Over 6 billion feet of timber was burned over an area larger than the states of Delaware and Rhode Island combined.

Street lights in Msisoula, 100 miles distant, were turned on early in the afternoon due to falling ashes and the dense smoke according to Harold B. Cain, retired assistant general manager for Mountain Bell and a former Missoula resident. The smoke reached as far as Denver, a thousand miles southeast.

Many accounts of rescue trips made by trains running from Wallace, Idaho to Superior and Missoula have been told. Located a few miles west of St. Regis, the towns of De Borgia, Haugan, Henderson and Taft were wiped out by the flames.

Mr. and Mrs. Richard M. Bell parents of Frank F. Bell, Montana public relations manager for Mountain Bell, Helena, were among those who escaped the flames by train.

The rescue train was boarded at Henderson where all local residents were employed at a sawmill owned by the Mann Lumber Company of Minneapolis Minn. Women and children were placed in boxcars while the men rode on flatcars loaded with piles of dirt and barrels of water, buckets and shovels.

From flatcars, water and dirt was thrown to the roofs of the boxcars as the train passed through the burning forests.. At Superior the train stopped along the Clark Fork river where pumps were available to drench the flaming roofs and sides of the wooden boxcars.

Household goods were buried at Henderson and DeBorgia prior to departure. Many residents of Missoula opened their homes to provide lodging for those arriving on trains. Mr. and Mrs. Bell stayed at the home of former Governor Joseph K. Toole at Missoula.

In July a fire fighting force of about 3,000 plus Army troops were engaged in preventing the spread of several thousand fires in Montana and Idaho. Winds of hurricane velocity swept the area in mid-August causing the small blazes to erupt into a major conflagration.

The fire crews and residents had to flee for their lives. About a third of Wallace, Idaho was burned leaving hundreds homeless. One account states, "During this time the telephone operators of the town stayed at their posts and gave free service to anyone who needed it".

Rain began falling during the last few days of August with snow in the higher elevations. Mother nature thus killed her own offspring.

Debries from Pulaski's tunnel

Photo courtsey of the Mineral County Historical Society

A Message from the International Association of Wildland Fire

The International Association of Wildland Fire is very pleased to have this opportunity to include a few words in this special commemorative edition of *The Big Burn*, being printed in recognition of the 100th anniversary of the 1910 fires in northern Idaho and western Montana.

The 1910 fires in the Northern Rocky Mountains were a precedent setting event and have since had far-reaching implications on how the wildland fire community and society as a whole views and deals with wildland fire regionally, nationally, and internationally. It seems only fitting that on the 100th anniversary of this historic event we reflect on lessons learned from the past as we implement innovative and contemporary best practices with managing wildland fires in the future.

Towards this end, the International Association of Wildland Fire will be holding its 3rd Fire Behavior and Fuels Conference in Spokane, Washington, October 25-29, 2010, to help commemorate the 100th anniversary of the 1910 fires. The theme of the conference is appropriately titled, "Beyond Fire Behavior and Fuels: Learning from the Past to Help Guide Us in the Future."

The International Association of Widland Fire is a non-profit, professional organization founded to promote a better understanding of wildfire, built on the belief that an understanding of this dynamic natural force is vital for natural resource management, for firefighter safety, and for harmonious interaction between people and their environment.

The association is dedicated to facilitating communication within the entire wildland fire community and providing global linkage for people with shared interest in wildland fire and comprehensive fire management. To learn more about the International Association of Wildland Fire, including the benefits of membership, visit our website (http://www.iawfonline.org/).

 International Association of Wildland Fire

*Facilitating **communication** and providing **leadership** for the wildland fire community*